ENDORSEMENTS

"I have known Clive Corfield for well over 35 years. I have watched him face extremely difficult and painful circumstances, as well as times of great blessing and triumph. Gifting and ability are important, and Clive is certainly a gifted and prophetic leader. However, the real measure of Godly leadership is character, integrity, faithfulness, trustworthiness and commitment to genuinely live out God's heart for people. As you carefully read each chapter of "Preparing the Bride", you will clearly see those things because that's who Clive is. It can be seen in everything he does. Clive is "the real deal" and I can highly recommend him to you!"

REV. DAN SNEED.
International Minister
Los Angeles, Cal. USA.

"A compassionate comment on the identity of the

Church to bring beautiful change in today's challenging times, as Clive paraphrases John 16:33, '...you will win because I have already won.' It's a message Clive Corfield lives with authenticity. I've witnessed Clive's uncompromising belief in the presence of Christ to save what is broken as he internationally equips the church, ministers restoration to ministers and powerfully delivers individuals from darkness. He believes in your ability to minister that freedom. My only problem writing an endorsement for this book? I was too busy being encouraged, spurred on and carried by its powerful potential."

LIZ EVANS
Love has a Voice
Prophetic Mentoring School Bristol, UK.

"Clive is straight talking, with great humour and yet profoundly prophetic, as he challenges and inspires us to encounter God afresh. There is such a huge sense of everything around us shifting and changing. This is especially true of the Church, as God is transforming us into a loving, living and intimate carrier of His presence. Clive helps us to understand the journey we are all on, whilst making sense of the shaking and biblically unpacking God's word. I encourage you to really take a hold of this amazing book as I know that as you do, you too will get a renewed vision of God's love for you, as part of His Bride being prepared for the return of her precious Bridegroom Jesus."

SUE SINCLAIR

"We are all heading to a Wedding — but that takes a particular preparation! Preparing the Bride by Clive Corfield takes a deep look at the Biblical principles involved in this process. Portraying the Father's heart, Clive's candid and sometimes humorous stories from his own journey help us recognise that everything we go through in this mortal life is a part of our training and spiritual formation. The Church needs such wise guidance from this seasoned equipper of the saints. The King is surely coming - let's get ready!"

DR. CLEM FERRIS
Itinerant Teaching and Prophetic Ministry
Governing Elder, Grace Church, Chapel Hill NC, USA.

"This book is a smorgasbord of prophetic and apostolic truth for such a times as this. Clive contextualises the work of the Holy Spirit in the Body of Christ and provides a scriptural route map we will be led along. The reader will experience a language that builds faith in the sophisticated and spiritual process of advancing. I wholly recommend Preparing the Bride for all believers whether in leadership or simply hungry for truth and seeking clarity on contemporary situations both inside

and outside the church."

REV. DR. ALAN ROSS.
Itinerant Teacher and Prophetic Ministry
Glasgow, Scotland.

"This book will challenge and remind you that it is not safe nor comfortable to be God's church, the bride of Christ. Clive Corfield unfolds how God's commission and call to be his church is to step into a destiny in which we not only experience the extravagant love of God but dare to challenge the tottering kingdoms of this world to embrace the radical lifestyle of the kingdom of Jesus."

REV. DR. RUSS PARKER
Author, Itinerant Ministry
England UK.

PREPARING THE BRIDE

Clive Corfield

To Karen, my bride.

CONTENTS

FOREWORD

As Solomon pointed out, "Beware... of the making of many books, there is no end!" If that was true in Solomon's day how much more today when so many have access to computers and all the self-publishing modes currently available. As Clive correctly points out in this excellent tome - there are many voices today confused between what's genuinely inspired and their own opinions!

My wife and I have been close friends and ministry associates of Clive and Karen for well over 25 years. Throughout those years, I have had a growing admiration of not only Clive's wisdom and perspectives but also his ability to state the timeless truths of God and life in fresh and easy to understand ways. *Preparing the Bride* not only exemplifies those abilities, but it also is chock full of what I would consider genuine prophetic insights for the Church today.

Often many books start with a rather vibrant compelling theme. Unfortunately you realize two thirds through some books, however, that most of the book is simply filler trying to reinforce that one beginning thought. Preparing the Bride, however, is thoroughly engaging chapter by chapter. There are so many helpful insights of wisdom they are too numerous to list. One, however, that I think will enlighten many, is Clive's clear distinction between the 'bride of Christ' and 'the body of Christ.'

While many use those titles almost as synonyms the reality is they point to two very distinct aspects of the church, which are essential to understand.

My biggest take away from this book, though, is Clive's stirring encouragement that we, the redeemed ones, are not here on earth simply to enjoy blessed lives. We are here by God's abundant grace to help give the nations to Christ as an inheritance AND become transformed into a beautiful eternal partner for the person of Christ Jesus!

MARC A. DUPONT
Mantel of Praise, San Diego, Cal. USA.

INTRODUCTION

As I look back on many years of pastoral work and itinerant ministry, I have noticed how at times Father God will put a burning message in your heart that is carried wherever you go and shared at every opportunity. It is both prophetic and relevant. Preparing the Bride is one such passionate message that burns within me to share with those who will listen.

I have held a series of one-day seminars on this subject in Lancaster, where we lived for 23 years, and I have preached it at many conferences and churches around the world. In 1999 I produced a booklet called *Preparing for Christ's Return*. It formed part of the 'Explaining Series' by Sovereign World Books. I have since continued to develop this theme as Holy Spirit gave me further revelation and I now believe it right to produce this book and make the teaching more widely available.

By way of information for those who have picked up this book and may be unfamiliar with some of the names of the characters that I will be referring to:

The Lamb is the Lord Jesus Christ, also known as the **Bridegroom.**
The Bride is the Church, those who are saved and know, love and live in relationship with the Lord Jesus Christ.

* * *

This book is about an event soon to take place: The return of Jesus Christ to this earth to take His Bride unto Himself, and the process of the Holy Spirit's work in preparing the Bride for this great event.

Preparing The Bride is not a book on eschatology or a prediction on current or forthcoming events within the world. It is an insight into what I understand the Holy Spirit to be doing today in preparing the Bride of Christ, the Church, for the coming of the Bridegroom, the return of the Lord Jesus Christ. I am therefore not offering my understanding on moons, dates, numerical conundrums or an interpretation of the world's political, ecological or sociological scenery. This offering, with God's help, is more to do with the internal development of the Bride, the Church, and its subsequent impact on the world. It is more concerned with vision, focus and Kingdom principles than being a "how-to" manual. Although I have spent a lot of my ministerial life teaching and training God's people for effective ministry, my hope is that this book stimulates thinking, discussion and helps refresh, focus and reform the shape of the Church in these end times, to be what God desires, designed and destined it to be.

* * *

Before I am able to get into the main thrust of the teaching and what I believe to be prophetic insight, it is necessary that I put everything into context. Hence the first chapter, "Unprecedented Days", will take a snapshot of the reality of who we are and where we are as the Church in todays world. "The Wedding of the Lamb" will open up the theme of the book further and lay the foundation for the main thrust of the teaching. "The Body and The Bride" will give some insight into these two contrasting terms which refer to the Church, revealing the essential nature of the message of this book. The remaining chapters are the crux of the matter, the core message of the book. I trust as I speak in general terms Holy Spirit will enable you to make them specifically relevant to you so that you may apply this message into your personal life and ministry.

* * *

The message within this book fits in very much with the current themes of renewal and the growing anticipation of revival within our nation. However, it may challenge our current perception of what we understand Holy Spirit is doing in preparing the Bride for Christ's return. There is so much talk about renewing love and intimacy with the Father and at the same time Father is turning lives upside down so we are no longer able to continue in the old ways. We are discussing new ways of doing church to become more relevant and effective, grappling with our theology on serious moral, ethical and social issues as cultures around us change faster than we can keep up with. There is a shaking going on, not only is our world changing beyond recognition but God is on the move, He is shaking our personal worlds, our church worlds and the political, social and religious worlds globally. God is on the move and He is shaking everything so that which is not of His kingdom will fall away and only that which is of His kingdom will remain. He is therefore working a renewing of our hearts and minds, drawing us back to Him, opening up our eyes to establish an unshakable faith in His fundamental truth and an emphasis of our lives and ministries that focus on the things of God's heart, His dream to be realised, our activities in line with and reflecting His agenda rather than repeating what we have always done and hoping He will bless our efforts.

It would appear that the moves of God over recent years have been a huge blessing for many. So much has been life re-leasing, essential in renewing our love and passion for God and healing up our broken lives. Whether we consider the Charis-matic Movement, Renewal, Father Heart, New Church or River Church etc., all were initiating and emphasising an aspect of God's love and power or experimenting with new ways of 'doing church'. While these movements have proved to be significant, in fact in some cases magnificent, glorious and highly impact-ing, they have, in the midst of the blessing and generous grace unfortunately created, in part, a rather self-centred, indulgent believer. Perhaps over fed on an abundance of teaching about how special we all are, our amazing destiny and unlimited po-tential, but with little or no teaching on service, suffering, ten-acity, disappointment, character and sacrifice. It seems only personal blessing is in vogue. However, the bible is full of men and women who lived in sacrifice and suffering, walking a road where a Sovereign God worked in and through them despite of them. Great victories and breakthroughs of course, but little in life is as instant, effortless and superficial as we would want. We are ourselves at risk of becoming, and therefore developing others to become, pampered children, where daddy loves us no matter what and will do whatever we want. Perhaps, in part, we have adopted the western pre-occupation with 'self' and 'ce-lebrity'. In our passion for releasing God's people from religious dogma and dead tradition we have gone to the other extreme and lean towards becoming ministerial superstars perform-ing sensational exploits. The tendency of successful churches now appears to be that they draw the hungry for God, willing but sometimes vulnerable and impressionable people, to join events or training schools which can become a bubble remote from reality. In these environments people are taught how to move naturally in the supernatural, which is great, but often equipped poorly for the harsh realities of life and operating as a true witness of Christ in the workplaces and communities in which they are placed. Jesus told us to go into the world to make disciples, true disciples who reflect Jesus and partner with the Holy Spirit in realising the dream of God.

Now I have to say I strongly believe in moving in the power of the Holy Spirit, healing, destiny, releasing potential and blessing etc. I believe the Lord is very much into all of this. However I equally believe Father God wants to bring a greater weight of maturity upon us, give us a clearer focus and a more holistic perspective of what it actually means to be in the Kingdom of God. We can then move on in our new found freedom and healing, taking true blessing, which is the Kingdom of God, to places where we can achieve the objectives, purposes and plans of God and be captivated by the Father and what truly lays on His heart. I believe we are in a time where it is essential to line up our lives and ministries with what is a priority to God and cooperate with Him as Holy Spirit prepares His Bride for the Bridegroom.

UNPRECEDENTED DAYS

P robably, like you, as a child I would often listen to the
grown-ups talking. I was born in 1954, only nine years
after the second world war, so there was often reflection
back to what it was like during those dark times.

I heard stories of bombs blowing out our front steps and
shards of glass from the window piercing the chair my dad was
sitting in just minutes before.

At the end of our garden was a disused air raid shelter in
which my brother and I would play and I remember being told
by our nan - "Don't go down that air raid shelter it may fall in
on your head!" I never really understood why anyone would put
trust in something to protect them from bombs that, by all accounts, may fall in on your head at any given moment!

I recall stories from my Dad, describing his life as a young
15 year old apprentice electrician working on a bitter cold
remote airfield, miles from home and suffering the abuse of
grumpy old sparks who gave him a hard time. When he finally
returned to London, he found himself working on the roof of
a building in the city when the air raid sirens went off and he
spotted a Doodle Bug approaching that seemed to be aiming
right for him. It was so funny listening to him tell the story of
how he didn't have time to get down so he ran around in cir-

cles not knowing what to do and then hitting the floor as it flew overhead and exploded nearby! Finally his war effort found him sent to the mines of North East England as a Bevin Boy, digging coal to fuel the ships and the ammunition factories. He actually wanted to join the navy but was ordered down the mines.

His brother, my uncle Ken, told elaborate stories of the big push into Europe, being bombed by Americans (known as friendly fire!) and hiding under an ammunition truck for shelter! Apparently on one occasion he was surrounded by a Panzer tank division, maybe the Americans were aiming for them. Nonetheless he did eventually get blown up by a member of his own troop playing around with a hand grenade. He was duly shipped home to recover. My brother and I used to feel the shrapnel that was left in his head and arm, gruesome really but it had to be done! A bit like when I had an operation and I took a photo of the wound just in case anyone wanted to see it. Nobody did really, but I was nevertheless proud of my bravery through the ordeal, which doesn't come that easy to me. Perhaps not quite in the same league as my uncle's shrapnel, I know, but it was my trophy of courage!

I remember many stories of what happened 'back in their day'. It was a time where my parent's generation were called up to do their duty. It was their day to rise up and be counted. I never cease to be amazed how they could find so much humour in such difficult and terrifying times.

When I was an apprentice electrician working on construction sites around London I would constantly hear the expression "when I was a lad.." or "when I was your age" or "back in my day" from the older tradesman. They all reflected back to when it was harder, grimmer, more challenging than us youngsters ever knew. "When I was your age I got up before dawn, cleaned out the fire grate, ate left over dog food and walked 20 miles to the pit in the pouring rain. I received a beating from the foreman and was then dropped down the pit shaft to make up for lost time." Although it's quite funny to reminisce about nowadays, it does highlight some of the attitudes of resentment that older generations can struggle with when considering how the world has, broadly speaking, become easier, more comfortable and more affluent for subsequent generations.

Perhaps the perception that the younger generation has it far too easy is true in some ways, but not all. Our five children, maybe like yours, have worked really hard to get their education, working their way through university doing horrible jobs at all hours of the day and night, struggling to make ends meet because we were not in a financial position to be of great financial support. Some have had to dig really deep to pursue success in their jobs, living in dreadful conditions, paying ridiculously high London rents and so on. Understandably the older generation remember the huge challenges they faced to achieve their successes and the struggles they endured just to survive. However they may feel, whilst the subsequent generations are not facing the same hardships as we did, in reality they do face their own unique challenges. They may be different to the obstacles we faced, but they are no less difficult. Social pressures, expectations and temptations are arguably far greater than any the older generations ever experienced.

I think those who want the younger generation to suffer 'like we did' reflect the attitude of the older brother in the story Jesus told of the lost son (Luke 15). He was so concerned with what he had done, how he had suffered, never abandoning his post on the farm but never feeling a son, accepted or belonging. An orphan if ever there was one. Striving, competing, proving self-worth, yet judging and criticising those who had found love, acceptance and grace without the need to do so.

So today is our day. It is not over yet. We may be older but we still have much to live for. It is still our day, especially if we pass something important on to the next generation. If you are young, your day is just dawning. It is foundation laying time. Embrace the experiences, make memories and aim high. Ultimately, this is the day the Lord has made, let us rejoice and be glad in it.

❈ ❈ ❈

I suggest every generation has lived through unprecedented days. Each has faced specific and unique challenges or obstacles that previous generations did not have to deal with, yet these challenges are no less difficult than those faced by generations before them. There is nothing new under the sun. Even though we live in an unsettled world full of threat, accelerated change in society's morality, values and aspirations, every generation has faced these same issues, though perhaps not at such an alarming rate as we do today. The development of science, whilst magnificent and by-and-large a massive contribution to human wellbeing, seems to produce a growing independence from God. Yet there has always been a leaning in the heart of man to be independent from God, for man to be his own master, even since the beginning when Eve was tempted by the serpent in the garden of Eden:

"For God knows that when you eat of it your eyes will be opened, and you will be like God...." (Gen 3:5)

The lure to be one's own God continued from the fall of man to the building of the tower of Babel and beyond. A vain attempt to reach God, or to be equal with God, be independent of God or be one's own God. The specific challenges alter but the nature of sin in the heart of man remains the same.

Similarly there is nothing new about the threat from other cultures upon our own. Through every generation the world has been plagued by the challenge of various strong, ambitious invading forces taking land not their own and subjecting the indigenous people to their rule. Empires have risen and fallen throughout recorded human history. Whether the ancient empires of Egypt, Babylon, Greece or Rome, or the more recent British and European empires, it is no different today than it has always been. The cycle remains the same, from conquest, subjection, imposition and inclusion to implosion, collapse or re-domination by a new stronger power.

Jesus certainly spoke of an increase of wars, rumours of wars, natural disasters and social turmoil as the final days approach. The apostle Paul, when he wrote to young Timothy, highlighted the social degeneration of the end times, reflecting the increase of unrestrained sin in the nature of human society.

"… People will be lovers of themselves, lovers of money, proud, abusive, disobedient to their parents, ungrateful, unholy, without love, unforgiving, slanderous, without self-control, brutal, not lovers of good, treacherous, rash, conceited, lovers of pleasure rather than lovers of God - having a form of godliness but denying its power.." (2 Tim 3:2-5).

While nothing is new, the intensity and rampant nature of unrestrained ungodliness does seem to be generally accepted by modern society as normal, even celebrated, rather than disapproved of and viewed as unacceptable. This would appear to highlight the reality of the days in which we are living, in the light of what Jesus announced would be the way of the world before He returns to earth (Matt 24).

Having said that I feel the need to remind us that it is not all doom and gloom. The ultimate victory is ours in Christ Jesus and reading the Bible we can clearly see that Jesus wins and that we have an eternal destiny which is glorious. However, I do need to put into context the reality of the situation we are living in so that the message of this book has greater relevancy and, hopefully, an encouraging and inspirational impact.

✽ ✽ ✽

A few years ago I was invited by my good friend Marc Dupont to share in a round table of prophetic, apostolic ministries at his home. I was so blessed and humbled to be in the midst of such gifted and anointed company. I struck up a conversation with Loren Sandford. I shared with him my growing desire to develop a teaching series on the theme of the prophetic church. To my amazement he produced the manuscript of his then latest book on this exact theme. The similarities of ideas and revelation were scary, though his were far more developed. However I felt this confirm my thinking or at least give confidence to what I believed God was speaking into my heart regarding the Church and the days in which we are living.

One of the concepts that has become popular over recent years is the idea of city transformation. The purpose being that we all work towards 'taking our cities for God.' The expectation is a complete transformation of our cities, in other words, seeing them won over and 'Christianised.' Although highly desirable, this concept is probably not very biblical and the idea seems to be more of a romantic notion that captures the imagination of passionate believers who are desirous for more to happen than they are seeing. This approach did seem to me more of a reflection of the nature of empire and triumphalism than the biblical understanding of the Kingdom of God. Particularly when held up to Jesus' own words in Matt. 24, much of the book of Revelation and many of the epistles, all of which paint a picture of the end times being dark and difficult. Hence, they urge courage, faithfulness and inspire strength in the midst of dreadful persecution. The relevancy of these teachings and revelations was specific to the church 2000 years ago, but it is also applicable for us today. I am not at all clear the bible speaks of an expansionist approach to taking over cities or the suggestion that society is completely changed by the impact of the Church. For sure history shows the Church has had great influence in social reform, introducing education, medicine, moral values, justice and shaping laws to establish righteousness. We have all benefited from those who pioneered and established much of what we enjoy in modern society. But, to my knowledge, there has never been a city that has been completely 'taken for Jesus' or remained in a permanent state of reform for subsequent generations. Great revivals throughout history have won many into the Kingdom of God and brought about a significant change to communities or influenced nations, but even these revivals have come, impacted significantly and then sadly faded.

Whilst considering the influence of the Church on society we must also understand the state of the Church in and of itself. It was once said - "you may preach measles but if you have mumps, that is what the people will get from you." The saying reflects the reality that we contaminate others not with what we say but with what we carry. Sadly, even in the Church, while we attempt to hold to a higher ideal of morality, integrity and righteousness, and even though we are saved, many still suffer with the same sinful condition of the heart. Our theology doesn't always align with our practical reality. Too often we preach beyond our experience and capability to perform.

I have spent a lot of time ministering to fallen pastors, helping them find their way back to God, attempting to rescue their marriages, families and congregations from the fallout. Helping those who have given themselves wholeheartedly yet with all integrity find themselves struggling with being abused by their congregations or suffering from burn out. There is of course also the celebrity culture of society which has gripped the Church, becoming part of its culture in many situations and standing in complete contrast to the teachings of Jesus about true leadership. If this is the condition of some of our leaders, then what is the true state of our congregations?

"The Church, must rise up to become what it purports to believe. This is my

passionate hope and prayer. Our image must align with our true identity, one of absolute integrity and spiritual reality."

The reality is that there is as much debt, adultery, greed, ambition, political control, crippling fear, depression, insecurity and dysfunction in the Church as there is outside of it in society. In many ways the world continues to influence the Church with its value system far more than the Church influences the world. The emotional and behavioural problems that constantly present in people are often resolved no more effectively inside the church than they are outside. I am persuaded beyond doubt that the Church will be built by the grace and power of God alone and not by any design or manufacture of man. Jesus promised that He would build the Church and the gates of hell would not be able to prevail against it. The church must rise up to become what it purports to believe. This is my passionate hope and prayer. Our image must align with our true identity; one of absolute integrity and spiritual reality.

There needs to be a serious intervention by God into the heart of the Church to bring about a radical transformation, a massive repentance and a significant healing and miracle of wholeness before we can ever touch our communities with anything like societal transformation.

C. H. Spurgeon said *"I believe that one reason why the church of God at this present moment has so little influence over the world is because the world has so much influence over the church."*

When Jesus prays His great intercessory prayer in John 17 His emphasis is on our protection from the evil one. This is because he, Satan, is the spirit of the power of the air who rules over this world's values and systems.

"Do not love the world or anything in the world. If anyone loves this world, the love of the Father is not in him." (1 Jn 2:15)

Satan hates us because we reflect the light and the glory of God

"For God who said 'let light shine out of darkness,' has made His light shine in our hearts to give us the light of the knowledge of the glory of God in the face of Jesus Christ." (2 Cor 4:6)

We are not of this world but of the Kingdom of Heaven. Therefore, we reflect, by grace, the nature of the divine, a very different spirit to that of the world. Jesus also prays that we may be one even as the Father and Son are one. Again, a unity, a oneness so integrated and complete that to observe it would prove difficult to see where one begins and the other ends. This being a very different spirit to that of the world who, by its own nature, works against unity between man and God and divides humanity on so many levels, not least of all within the Church.

Jesus finally encourages His followers with these words:

"I have told you these things, so that in me you may have peace. In this world you will have trouble. But take heart! I have overcome the world." (Jn 16:33)

Effectively Jesus was saying; it's going to be a tough battle with the world, but you will win, because I have already won. The winning or overcoming has to mean the Church not coming under the world's influence, values and demands, but rather seeking to influence the world with Kingdom values just as salt, light and yeast influences its environment. We occupy, seek to be faithful, fruitful and a means through which heaven comes to earth until He returns.

Isaiah prophesied, *"Arise, shine, for your light has come, and the glory of the Lord rises upon you. See darkness covers the earth and thick darkness is over the peoples, but the Lord rises upon you and His glory appears over you. Nations will come to your light, and kings to the brightness of your dawn."* (Isa. 60:1-3)

I believe in these final days as we wait with a strong desire for Jesus to return, the world will get darker and darker. Yet I believe the Church will grow brighter and brighter. There will be a clear contrast between the light and the dark as the light glows brighter against the backdrop of darkness.

When a jeweller presents diamonds to a customer, they often put them on a black cloth so that the diamond can be seen clearer against the dark background. This is how Christ will be seen in the Church against the dark backdrop of the world. The Light of the world will shine and be made brighter, clearer, more obvious, unavoidable in contrast to the environment which surrounds it.

"There is a growing contrast between Kingdom communities and religious establishments, both within ancient traditions and more modern, contemporary expressions of the church."

I expect Holy Spirit to raise up communities of God's people, Church in its various expressions, who are bearers of His presence. Loren Sandford uses the phrase "Islands of glory in a sea of mud." I love this phrase and have sometimes used it to illustrate what I believe God is doing today.

There is a growing contrast between Kingdom communities and religious establishments, both within ancient traditions and more modern, contemporary expressions of the church. Mud is water filled with pollutants and contaminated with debris and much of the Church does appear to be 'muddy' on a number of issues. Often what is seen to be church sociologically is a mixture of worldliness and vague spirituality. Generally speaking, the Church has not given a clear message of right or wrong, of what God desires or what our focus and emphasis should be in accordance with what the Holy Spirit is saying and doing today.

Among those who are open to Him the move of the Spirit today is initiating a raising up of lighthouse churches from among the muddy waters of compromise and worldly self-interest. These communities will reveal who and what Father God is like. His tangible presence will be the priority of these communities and God will be evidently manifest in their midst. These 'Islands of Glory' will give proper place to the Holy Spirit to lead and shape who and what they are meant to be according to Father's design. They will be wholly bent on realising the Father's vision and line up with His agenda, rather than fulfilling the dictates, preferences and traditions that express man's control and desires. These communities, by nature, will be highly prophetic. Not wacky or sensation seeking for the sake of it but deeply tuned into and sensitive to the Holy Spirit.

I would understand that these islands will be communities held together in meaningful relationship where the honour of God and one another is a cultural priority. They will be places where the atmosphere and practice will be one of healing the whole person, spirit, soul and body, from all pain, wounding and damage from sin, Satan and self. Where we have become so messed up, bruised and beaten by life's experiences, here we will find healing in a home. Not a place to attend, but a place to belong and discover a safe environment where we can grow and become all that we are designed and destined to be. A place of prophetic hope, a beacon on a hill shining like a lighthouse to warn off danger and welcome those attracted to what we offer.

All of this may sound idealistic and not very pragmatic, perhaps it is, but what else do we envisage the Church being? We must be careful not to default to a religious social club or an empty shell of irrelevant religious activity that is neither transforming its own people into wholeness or holiness nor impacting society. Our church practice may be done with deep sincerity, heartfelt loyalty and faithfulness but it has the potential to become an old wineskin, unable to contain the new wine of God.

Now it has to be acknowledged that the Church has been a truly remarkable vehicle for societal change. It has also been, through its many expressions, the sole vessel for preserving, proclaiming and advancing the gospel worldwide. The Church is the Body of Christ, the 'called out' ones, the Bride being prepared for the Bridegroom. In the light of this we should love, honour and embrace, as well as celebrate all that has been achieved through it to date. However, we are living in unprecedented times, in that it is our watch, our time to develop upon what has been and lay fresh foundations for subsequent generations. We are responsible for our responses to what the Holy Spirit is saying today and, in turn, our actions will have a bearing on how the kingdom advances and what the next generation has available to build upon.

So, the challenge arises, what are we working towards and building up? If we do not line up with God's dream, His vision, then we build our own empire, potentially impregnating it with the values of the world. These foundations will be weak and not those of the Kingdom of Heaven. Even so we may still have the audacity to ask God to bless it!

'Change is essential and this will take courage as well as patience, yet only a radical and audacious approach will shift the entrenched and inspire those who are not so much critical or judgemental but have a cry in their hearts that sings

"there has to be more than this!"'

The reality is that we can only ever begin from where we are, and we can only ever build with the materials currently available to us. Therefore abandoning our churches as they are now will only achieve disillusionment, heartache and division. However, a positive, intentional move to embrace the voice of God and become the prophetic Church is essential. What this looks like in practice will be interesting to discover, but I am confident it will be far more organic than organisational, less corporate and more relational.

I believe the journey starts with capturing the heartbeat of God and His agenda is for us today, recognising that it will be that same as it has always been in terms of values and objectives but noting that the expression and emphasis will resonate with the rhythm of heaven and a fresh relevancy to contemporary society. Change is essential and this will take courage as well as patience, yet only a radical and audacious approach will shift the entrenched and inspire those who are not so much critical or judgemental but have a cry in their hearts that sings "there has to be more than this!"

The underlying actions and purposes of God today are, in general, the same as they have always been and this is revealed in part when he speaks to His people in the wilderness.

"You yourselves have seen what I did to Egypt, and how I carried you on eagles wings and brought you to myself ... out of all the nations you will be my treasured possession. Although all the earth is mine, you will be for me a kingdom of priests and a holy nation..." (Ex 19:5-6)

Here we see God's desire to redeem a body of people from among the nations of the earth, deliver them from the hand of the enemy, draw them unto Himself as His treasured possession and form them into a Kingdom of priests and a holy nation. His intent is always to rescue, rebuild, value and create a people for His purpose who reflect, represent and express Him.

"This creation, the Church, is designed, established and empowered for Him and by Him to realise His dream and to reflect His glory."

Genesis 1:28 reveals that God has designed us to be blessed, fruitful, to increase and to rule. We do this in the knowledge that we, the redeemed of God, are participators in His great, unfolding story.

The first two chapters of Ephesians never stop blowing my mind. The unfolding revelation of how we are included in the developing story of God. In verse 7 of chapter 2 the apostle Paul says:

"In order that in the coming ages He might show the incomparable riches of His grace, expressed in His kindness to us in Christ Jesus."

Somehow, in His grace, limitless wisdom and power He demonstrates through us His riches, nature, character and overwhelming kindness. We become His trophy in which He delights. Verse 10 affirms this:

"For we are God's workmanship, created in Christ Jesus to do good works, which God prepared in advance for us to do."

This creation, the Church, is designed, established and empowered for Him and by Him to realise His dream and to reflect His glory.

Nothing has changed. God is building His Church according to His plans and purposes. Our responses will be either contributively helpful or obstructive. Hence hearing clearly from God is vital for us if we are to keep in step and in line with His process and play our part well.

Today, just as we have seen historically, there are many voices claiming to be speaking on behalf of God. Much of what is broadcast as prophetic may be an expression of personal opinion, preference, theological or political stance or even a compulsion to be heard or needed. There may often be a pressure for those recognised as having a prophetic voice to perform and come up with something that is topical. I am reminded of Jeremiah and other great prophets of God who had to be clear and deliver the word of the Lord through a fog of false prophets who were only saying what the people wanted to hear. God's word may not always be popular; it may not be in vogue or in line with current trends or modern culture, but when God speaks those with ears to hear will hear what the Spirit is saying to the church (Rev 2:11,17, 29; 3:6, 13, 22). Hopefully we will respond with due diligence and fervour.

THE WEDDING OF THE LAMB HAS COME

The Wedding of the Lamb

R evelation 19 begins with a resounding chorus of the multitude of heaven shouting:

"Hallelujah! Salvation and glory and power belong to our God!"

The host of heaven were rejoicing over the destruction of the great prostitute, Babylon. We see significant personalities in heaven bowing down and worshipping God who is seated on the throne, a great multitude crying out:

"Hallelujah! For our Lord God Almighty reigns."

In verse 7 we read:

"Let us rejoice and be glad and give Him glory! For the wedding of the Lamb has come and His bride has made herself ready. Fine linen, bright and clean, was given her to wear. (Fine linen represents the righteous acts of the saints) *Then the angel said to me "Write: 'Blessed are those who are invited to the wedding supper of*

the Lamb!'" And he added, "These are the true words of God."

We see three main concepts in this passage and throughout this book I will seek to unpack each of these themes in turn.

1) The wedding of the Lamb has come.
2) The Bride has made herself ready.
3) Blessed are those who are invited to the wedding.

Wherever I travel around the world there appears to be a heightened excitement and anticipation about the return of the Lord Jesus. This event, known as the *'parousia'*, which speaks of Christ's return - the literal, physical presencing of Himself with us - is spoken of repeatedly throughout scripture and is the great hope of the Church. Now, as never before, there seems to be the dawning of the reality of this event.

We may fall out with each other, as theologians have done down through the centuries, about the sequence, timing, and detailed understanding of Jesus' return but one thing is certain – Jesus is coming back again as a bridegroom for His bride, and those who are living in relationship with Him, through salvation, are part of the bride.

The Three-Stage Process to Marriage

Culturally speaking, when Jesus walked this earth there were three stages to marriage. The first stage was 'betrothal', which was a legal agreement between the couple who were intending to marry. Even up until one generation ago, when a man asked a young woman to marry him and she agreed, they became engaged or betrothed. This was a legally binding contract and if the man chose not to go through with the wedding it was possible for the girl to sue him for breach of contract. Therefore, we need to see marriage, beginning at the time of betrothal, as legal and binding. This gave security and assurance to the parties involved, sealing the relationship until the fulfilment of the forthcoming event, - marriage.

The second stage was the coming of the bridegroom for his bride. We see this illustrated in Matthew 25 where Jesus tells the story of the parable of the virgins. In verse 6 we read:

'At midnight the cry rang out: "Here's the bridegroom! Come out to meet him!"'

At this point the virgins, who were sleeping, woke up, trimmed their lamps and went out to meet the bridegroom to form the complete wedding party.

This led to the third stage, which was the wedding feast, - the actual joining of a husband and wife together and the accompanying celebration. The book of Revelation refers to this event taking place when the Church experiences the wedding supper of the Lamb!

"Then the angel said to me, "Write: 'Blessed are those who are invited to the wedding supper of the Lamb!'" (Rev 19:9).

This three-stage process is also taking place in the lives of individual believers. First of all, from the moment we are saved there is a betrothal between Jesus and ourselves. When we give our lives to Him and submit to His Lordship, accept His forgiveness and cleansing through the power of the cross, He enters into a legal contract with us. He says:

"I will never leave you nor forsake you, I will be with you always, I will come again for you."

We see this in John 14. Jesus encourages us not to let our hearts be troubled but to trust in God and to trust in Him. When we are saved Jesus comes into our lives and we are sealed into Him. This relationship is legally binding, a covenant that is signed with the blood of Jesus and the promise from Him that He will come back for us.

The second stage of the process of marriage is the coming

of the bridegroom for his bride. I believe this to be the return of the Lord Jesus from heaven to earth to take His bride, the Church, unto Himself.

The third stage is the completion of the marriage process. At the actual joining of the husband and wife, referred to as 'the wedding supper of the Lamb,' there will be a great celebration beyond our wildest dreams. We can only imagine what this wedding celebration will be like, but I know that it will be far more glorious and wonderful than anything we have ever experienced here on earth.

* * *

By way of illustration, let me tell you a little about my marriage to Karen. Well, I probably need to explain that Karen took me on along with my three children, Laura who was then 8, Sarah 6 and Ben 3 years old. I had been on my own with the children for a few years and knew deep in my heart I would marry again. The children needed a mum and I needed a wife. I had taken the children with me to Los Angeles to stay with my good friends Dan and Bev Sneed who were a safe place of refuge and healing for me. During this time, I received a word from a minister friend that the next Mrs Corfield would, in part, be chosen by my children. I know my kids loved to watch the movie '*Chitty, Chitty, Bang, Bang*'. I think they saw me as the mad professor. Our home was a little like that to be honest and I didn't mind the thought that a Truly Scrumptious may be their choice of mother! Well, she was pretty and she did come from a money family... Just kidding!

Once I returned to the England, I went to visit some good friends in Hereford. I knew they had a grown-up daughter called Karen although I had never met her. Well up until this visit that is. Unfortunately, I didn't make a good first impression. I was sitting in their garden with my overcoat on. I was cold even though it was mid-summer in England. The weather in California in August is remarkably hot compared to where I now found myself. I am told that when Karen came home, she looked out of the window and said to her mother, "who is the idiot in the garden wearing a coat in this weather?" Not such a good start. Apparently, Jeanette, Karen's mother, went upstairs and looked out at me in the garden and heard the audible voice of God say "this is the man your daughter will marry." I was only told this many years later. However, when I first met Karen, I was instantly attracted to her but felt I had very little to offer her so did not pursue her in any way. I have to say that it was not easy for me but I felt it was important to be willing to temporarily let her go in order to see if God was involved in this.

Some time later Jeanette called me to see if I would like to join them on holiday along with her younger children, whose ages were similar to that of my own. I agreed excitedly because having fun is quite a high priority in my life! Then I was told, "Oh, by the way, Karen will be joining us if that is okay?" I played it cool of course. "That's fine," I said. "The more the merrier."

We all arrived in convoy at the caravan park in Cornwall and began a happy holiday. What I quickly noticed, without any prompting from me or anyone else, was how my children began to relate to Karen. There was lots of hair brushing and girly talk. My children made pictures of flowers and stuck them on the outside of her bedroom window so that when she woke up and drew open her curtains there was a picture looking back at her. I began to feel my way forward to see if there would be a positive response by stopping the car in a lane and picking wild flowers from the car window and handing them to Karen sitting beside me. I looked in the rear-view mirror to see the kids giggling and looking pleased at all this. One day on the beach, Karen, who was a gymnast, was showing the children how to do back flips, cartwheels and other such things. After her incredibly good demonstration of a series of rather professional hand springs and flips the children in their glee and desire for me to be a hero, shouted "Come on Dad, you do some!" The thought of being upside down in mid-air didn't really appeal to me so not wanting to disappoint the children or humiliate myself, I told them that my back was feeling a bit stiff, otherwise I would obviously have obliged.

The holiday continued until I plucked up the courage and asked Karen's dad, Mel, if he would be okay with me taking Karen out for a drink and whether he and Jeanette would look after the children for me while we were out. To my surprise he seemed quite keen on the idea and said that they would be happy to babysit. So, off we went for the evening for a drink in a local fishing village pub. It was a lovely evening, we got along really well, chatting, laughing, occasionally touching hands on the table. On the way back to the car we walked around the quayside looking at the reflection of the moon in the water and feeling the warm breeze flowing across the water. In actual fact there was what appeared to be some smuggling going on, some shifty characters were loading things from a small boat into a van whilst constantly checking around! I was trying to steer Karen away from what looked like seriously dodgy dealings, but she wanted to have a closer look to see what they were doing! I should have known then she was fearless, inquisitive and altogether adventurous.

I managed to lead her away from the potential danger back to the car and then back to the caravan. Everyone was asleep, we sat down together and I knew I needed to make a manly move to kiss her but my confidence was seriously lacking. I suddenly couldn't remember how to kiss. Do you suck? Do you blow? What if I move forward and she turns away and I end up kissing the cushion by her head! Oh, the stress of being romantic! After much talk, which was probably waffle from me trying to fill the time, I took a deep breath and went in for my best move, lips poised, eyes open to start with to get my aim right, then closing them upon impact at the last moment. Joy! Lip on lip contact first time. "What a star you are Corfield" I thought to myself. Then I realised the kiss was not only being accepted but reciprocated with tender affection. "You've scored mate," I said delightedly in my head. At least I hope it stayed in my head!

Well that was the beginning of our relationship. A year later I asked Mel for his daughter's hand in marriage and he gave me his permission and blessing. I had casually asked the children what they would think if Karen came in to our home and became their new mum. I think from that time on they chose to call her mummy Karen until the wedding, then they chose to call her mum. I think they were part of the whole process of our relationship's development.

The night I proposed was Karen's birthday. I had no money whatsoever but prayed for God to confirm His blessing upon Karen and I by asking for the miracle of an engagement ring. That night two anonymous cash gifts, sealed in envelopes, were put through our letter box, just enough to cover the cost of a ring for her. I was so overwhelmed at God's grace and favour.

I wanted Karen to understand what marrying me would potentially be like, so in the restaurant, while celebrating her birthday, I took out the miracle ring and said something along these lines: "Karen, I don't have any money, I am in debt, I have gone through a dreadful divorce, I am a pastor nobody wants to employ at the moment, I only want to serve Jesus and I am willing to travel anywhere, do anything to obey him. I can offer no material security, I am ten years older than you and I have three kids. I don't have much to offer you other than my heart and absolute devotion. I want you to join me on this mad adventure of faith by being my wife. Will you please marry me? She smiled openly and said yes! I was so surprised at her immediate response, so I started my speech again as I thought she hasn't quite understood what I was offering! "Karen, I don't have any money, I am in debt.........." "Yes" she said, "I will marry you." Well I was one happy preacher in that restaurant. My dream had come true, the love of my life had agreed to partner with me for life. Now we had to go back and announce this to our family.

We arrived back at Karen's family home, a beautiful farm in Herefordshire. We walked in and I asked for everyone to gather in the kitchen area so that I could make an announcement. "I have asked Karen to marry me and she has agreed to do so", at which point all the children, both my own and Karen's younger brothers, giddily charged around the house laughing and telling each other who they would be in relationship to one another! "You're my uncle", "You will be my niece," and so on. And so our new family was born, often known as 'team family' to this day. It has expanded considerably as Karen and I went on to have two children of our own, Joshua and Kathryn. They are all grown up now and away from home. University, careers, weddings, grandchildren, we have been so blessed by God, seriously blessed beyond measure. Last year our eldest daughter Laura came home from New Zealand where she now lives with her family and we all went on a family holiday together. Five generations of one family hanging out for a week. How cool is that?

* * *

It is such a wonderful thing to be chosen and accepted, to be loved, valued and to belong. What a privilege it is to be chosen to be part of the Bride of Christ. As a man, I find it quite difficult to imagine myself as a bride, especially the part that involves wearing a frilly white dress and walking down the aisle! The whole concept of being a bride can be difficult for men to grasp because of its feminine implications. However, if we can view it from the perspective that Jesus wants and loves us more than anything else in His creation and doesn't want to continue on into eternity without us, this will give us some idea of the depth of His love, commitment and desire for us all.

As I explained earlier, when I first met Karen it wasn't long into our acquaintance that I began to realise how I wanted to spend more of my time in her company than in the company of others. As time progressed the desire in my heart for her far outweighed any practicality that may have been a hindrance or an obstacle. When I arrived at the point of not wanting to live without her I asked her to marry me, and to my delight she accepted. From that very moment we were betrothed, committed to one another, convinced we were right for each other. Therefore, we launched into planning and preparing for the wedding day itself. When the wedding day arrived we met at the church, made our public vows before God and man and then entered into the celebration of the wedding reception. After that we went off to start our new life together as one. As the Apostle Paul says in Ephesians 5, talking about marital relationships:

'For this reason a man will leave his father and mother and be united with his wife, and the two will become one flesh. This is a profound mystery - but I am talking about Christ and the Church."

It seems that marriage on earth is a prophetic illustration of what is yet to take place between Christ and His Church. At this stage we are betrothed to Him and He promises to return for us and take us into the marriage supper of the Lamb; to become one and be complete with Him. For me, as for many others, it is a great mystery that God would love me to the point of wanting to be in relationship with me, - I would be grateful just to have eternal life and not be facing the prospect of hell. It is incredible to me then that we have been saved so that God might pour into us His love and blessings, just as a loving bridegroom would want to love and cherish his new wife.

The Birthing of the Bride

The Genesis account of Adam and Eve offers far more than the story of the origins of man and his subsequent adventures with God. In Genesis 2:7 we read that Adam was created from the dust of the earth. I believe this to mean that we, as humans, are created out of the same basic material as the rest of creation, designed to be one with and integral to the natural realm.

Adam must have been one whole being containing both male and female natures, reflecting the entire and complete image and likeness of God, who, Himself, is both male and female. Jesus always referred to the Almighty as His Father, a male title, but recognised the female nature of the divine, sighting that the Spirit gives birth to spirit, birthing being a female capability alone. Jesus Himself brooded over Jerusalem like a hen broods over her chicks, again reflecting the mother nature of God.

Therefore, Adam had wrapped up in his being the whole nature, image and likeness of God. Adam was placed in Eden to work and take care of God's creation. He had the breath (Holy Spirit) of God blown into his nostrils and became a living being or living soul. His natural, material part infused with self-consciousness capable of thinking, feeling and making moral choices; a complete personality.

However, God saw that it was not good for man to be alone (Gen 2:18). Even though Adam was perfect, a reflection of the divine and in harmonious union with God, he still appeared to have an unmet need. Adam needed a partner, a helper suitable for him. The story tells us that God caused Adam to go into a deep sleep (v21), He took part of Adam, the female element, and formed woman from this. Eve was in all respects part of a whole but a specific expression of that which was once wrapped up entirely within Adam. Now there was one being identifiable in two separate forms, Adam and Eve, yet each maintained the integrity of the original whole. We know that they were now able to procreate and produce offspring, bearing their own DNA, to perpetuate their seed. Yet each child would hold their own unique God created personality.

Jesus was known as the second Adam. When Jesus died on the cross and was buried, it reflected the first Adam being put into a deep sleep. When Jesus rose from the dead, as the first Adam rose from his sleep, - a type of resurrection, - he was given a woman, Eve. So too Jesus had a bride given to Him following His resurrection, the Church. The word "church" literally means the "called out" ones. The Church comprises those who are called out of the world unto Christ through salvation.

Now a new body (of Christ) is created to reflect the female counterpart of the second Adam, Christ Jesus. Additionally, this new female body is able to receive the seed of Christ. Jesus is known as the Word of God (John 1:1) and we know that the Word is referred to as seed (Luke 8:11). As the seed, Christ, enters into the lives of those who, by faith, believe and receive Him, the supernatural work of the Holy Spirit produces new spiritual birth in them and they become new sons of the Father. All these true sons have within them the divine attributes capable of procreation. The Church becomes the Bride of Christ, the object of Divine love, and out of this intimate love union true sons of the Father are born. These sons are disciples who, in turn, spread the divine seed of light and life, enabling Holy Spirit to bring about new birth, making other disciples and thus perpetuating the expansion of the Church, the Bride of Christ.

❊ ❊ ❊

This does of course bring fresh insight into the place of women in the Church. Right from the beginning women had equal stature with man. Different roles of course, yet utterly inter-dependant upon and beautifully complimenting one another. Together they form a oneness in the image and likeness of God through their unique differences, emotionally and physiologically, for the roles each were created to perform.

The subjection of women to the subordination of man came about as a result of the curse that was put upon them following their fall in the garden (Gen 3:16). Therefore, we must understand that the subjection of women to male dominance is a result of the fall and not the original design of God, thus rendering the relationship between men and women dysfunctional, operating under curse rather than the intended blessing. If the cross is God's means of salvation for humanity, then through the power of the cross we have the means to restore relationships back to their original condition, position and function. If this is the case, and I believe it to be so, then the Church should be the one place on earth where woman have their rightful place restored through the redemptive power of the cross. As it was in the garden, so it should be in the Church today because

"Christ has redeemed us from the curse of the law.." (Gal 5:13)

In Christ we are no longer under curse therefore both men and women can stand in their rightful place as partners with equal authority, expressing their unique roles without seeking to subject or usurp one other.

Restoring men and women back to the original design, plan and purpose of God must also mean that gender roles are restored through the redemptive power of the cross. Jesus made it clear when He quoted Genesis 1:26:

"In the beginning of creation God made them male and female".

There doesn't seem to be much confusion in God's original creative order. Since the fall in the Garden of Eden there has been an opening up of sin and death which has brought into humanity and the whole of creation a perversion and contamination that has rendered a developing crisis in identity, gender and relationship roles. Jesus said:

'Have you not read that the one who made them at the beginning "made them male and female", and said, "For this reason a man shall leave his father and mother and be joined to his wife, and the two shall become one flesh"? So they are no longer two, but one flesh. Therefore what God has joined together, let no one separate.' (Matt 19:4-6)

This is why it is so important to understand that God created us male and female with intentionality and for a purpose, and that purpose is to reflect who and what He is like in His entirety. True marriage is a prophetic foretaste of Christ (male) and the Church (female) coming together in perfectly designed unity. Man was intentionally designed to become one flesh with woman; woman, likewise, is fashioned to be complete and compatible with man. In this respect, same sex relationships undermine the purposive nature of our existence, at best presenting an ambiguous and confused representation of God, and at worst perverting our view of Him altogether.

Over many years of pastoral ministry, I have sought to minister to a number of God's people who have been in torment over their sexual identity or have battled with strong same sex desire. Their journey has not been easy. Some have made lifestyle choices and chosen to believe, with sincerity, that their sexual identity is their gift from God. Others have wilfully defied Gods word and embraced a lifestyle contrary to scripture, even with a sure knowledge of the biblical stance. Sadly they will reap the consequences of those choices, as scripture says;

"Do not be deceived: God cannot be mocked. A man reaps what he sows." (Gal 6:7)

Still others who have recognised that their condition is a flaw, the result of the fall and its subsequent effect upon us all, have accepted Gods design for humanity and His way of redemption through the cross. Salvation, including forgiveness, healing and deliverance are available for those who believe. Sexual sin, inner torment or feeling confused about who and what we are, is no different to greed, pride, hatred or rebellion. We sin and we can be sinned against resulting in rejection, fear and emotional damage. Even if we suffer from a physical malfunction or disability, and most of us do to greater or lesser degrees, it is all the effect of sin and death upon humanity.

The cross of Jesus is God's means of salvation to restore all things back to its original condition in the Garden of Eden. Ultimately when Jesus returns all things will be made new. A new heaven and a new earth. He will wipe away every tear from our eyes. There will be no more crying or pain for the old corrupted order will pass away and He makes everything new! (Rev 21:1-5). Until that time we have been commissioned and empowered as true sons of God to advance the Kingdom of God by making disciples, healing the sick and setting captives free by all means available to us. Jesus said;

"The thief (Satan) comes to kill and to destroy but I have come that they may life, and have it to the full" (John 10:10).

It would be better not to accept a flaw in our lives as a gift from God or wrap our identity in our imperfections. Rather embrace the acceptance of God for who we are in essence and allow Him to work healing, restoration and cleansing, enabling our true self in Christ to find expression and fulfilment.

The birthing of the Bride is a marvellous miracle initiating a body of 'called out' ones journeying from darkness to light, from death to life, realising the purpose of God and forming a dynamic body reflecting the Divine.

Paul put it well when he gave account of his call and commission to Agrippa. In quoting what Jesus had spoken to him directly:

"To open their eyes and turn them from darkness to light, and from the power of Satan to God, so that they may receive forgiveness of sins and a place among those who are sanctified by faith in me." (Acts 26:18)

This has to be our call and commission also. To experience full salvation and to minister full salvation to all those who are open to receive.

THE BODY AND THE BRIDE

Understanding the nature and purpose of the Church.

Perhaps the best place to start is with what I believe to be a prophetic insight into the work of Holy Spirit today in preparing the Church for the return of the Lord Jesus Christ. We need to establish exactly what we mean by 'the Church' and the different terms relating to it and, additionally, we may find that we need to change the way we think of church to help us line up with the plans and purposes of God.

Romans 12:1-2 ushers in a tremendous challenge to the way that we live and think. God, through the apostle Paul, pleads with us to present ourselves as:

"Living sacrifices, holy, pleasing to God - this is our spiritual act of worship."

We are also instructed:

"Do not conform any longer to the pattern of this world, but be transformed by the renewing of your mind. Then you will be able to test and approve what God's will is - His good, pleasing and perfect will."

There is an important word in this sentence. It is the word

'then'. It would appear that to know God's perfect will and purpose we must first present ourselves as living sacrifices, holy and pleasing to God. This in itself is a challenge, yet we are also urged not to conform to the pattern of this world but to be transformed by the renewing of our minds. THEN we will be in a better position to see and hear God clearly and we are more likely to respond in the way that Holy Spirit requires of us.

There is a work of God in our lives that necessitates Him bringing about a complete change in our thinking, perception and approach to what His plans and purpose actually are. For us to see or understand what God is up to we have to view things from His perspective. In my training course "Issues of the Heart and Mind" I look into this in far more detail. However, for our purposes here it is sufficient to say that we need to change our minds about how we approach and 'do' church and what we understand it to be.

Considering the phrase *'do not conform to the pattern of this world'* we become aware that there is a way that the world does things and a way that God does things. They are not the same. Another way of saying 'do not conform' is to say 'don't be put into the same mould as the world, don't let it shape you or your thinking.' The word 'conform' in the language that the New Testament was written in is *'suschematizo'* and it means 'to fashion alike,' i.e. adhere to the same pattern.

When I was a child, like most children I loved jelly. I used to help make it and the process was very simple. All you needed to do was put jelly cubes in a bowl, add boiling water, pour the mixture into a jelly mould and allow to cool before putting it into the fridge to set. After a while we took it out of the fridge and tipped the mould upside down onto a plate. To our delight the jelly wobbled on the plate in the shape of the mould we had used. Well, more often than not, as there were occasionally disasters, however, the point is that the jelly took on the shape of the mould and remained that way thereafter.

We are urged not to conform to the ways of the world, its values, ambitions and practices, but encouraged in this passage to *"be transformed by the renewing of the mind."* Now this term 'transformed' is *'metamorphoo'* and it is the same word from which we derive the English word metamorphosis. It is describing a complete change, like that of a caterpillar changing into a butterfly and has a completely different meaning to *'suschematizo'* described above. One is to mould you into its own ways, the other is to change you from one thing into another. All the ingredients and essence of what you are to become are already contained within you but it is through the transformational process that the old dies away and the new emerges, just like the butterfly. The intent is always for the butterfly to emerge. It would be daft to cram a load of caterpillars into a butterfly shaped mould and expect it to become a real, living, beautiful butterfly. Each caterpillar has to be transformed into what it was designed to be. Likewise, we must break out of the moulding that the world puts upon us and instead allow Holy Spirit to transform us through the renewing of our minds. It is this transforming of our minds that is key to our personal, and therefore corporate, transformation.

Jesus opened up His earthly ministry with this statement:

"The time has come, the kingdom of God is near. Repent and believe the good news!" (Mark 1:15)

The word repent simply means to change your mind, to stop thinking the way we do and stop believing what is a lie. The battleground is so often in the mind. What we believe, the way we understand or perceive things will always produce a feeling, which in turn dictates our behaviour.

Jesus said that the Kingdom of God is near, so stop thinking the way that you do, don't be conformed into the pattern of this world, start believing the good news! It is through this heavenly revelation that Jesus brings good news. This revelation is the power that liberates our minds from darkness to light, from lies to truth. Jesus said that we will know the truth and the truth will set us free and this liberating truth is life transforming. As our minds are renewed by this truth, we transform from what we once were into what God designed us to be from the very beginning of time.

This same principle has to be applied not only to us as individuals but also to the Church. The way that we think, make decisions, what we value, how we understand ourselves, what we do etc., these things are either shaped by the pattern of this world or are a reflection of heaven here on earth.

By way of teasing this out further let me offer a broad generalisation. For many Pentecostal and Evangelical churches the purpose of the church is to be a sort of discipleship factory. There is an emphasis on reaching out to the unchurched and by all means bringing as many as possible into their fold. Once we have won them we train them to go out and bring others in, and by and large this is the general pattern of things. Without doubt Jesus told us in the Great Commission (Matt 28) to go into all of the world and make disciples of all nations. So winning people to Jesus is of course a wonderful thing, however I am not convinced that getting people into our churches and making disciples are one and the same thing at all. I have spent much of my ministerial life seeking to win people to Jesus and equipping God's people to do likewise. I am therefore utterly committed to winning people to Him, helping form them into Christ and enabling them to become effective disciples of Jesus.

* * *

Some of the early attempts of what we once called 'soul winning' may have left scarring on my soul, or at least a very deep memory, hopefully offset now by a wisdom of how not to do things!

When I gave my life to Christ back in 1975 I had experienced a transforming conversion and was very keen to be a true disciple of Jesus. I was raised with a church upbringing but had slid far away from God, church and my family. After being caught up in all kinds of unhealthy and unholy living I ended up suffering a nervous breakdown, crippled with all kinds of fears. By God's amazing grace He delivered and healed me quite dramatically and set me on a road of recovery. During those early, vulnerable years I joined a church near East Croydon where the pastor was fired up and desperate for us all to reach the lost in our city. The motive was good, but the practice was dreadful.

On one attempt to save the city we were all instructed to assemble at the church so that we could embark on a walk of witness. I have to say I had major reservations on a number of levels, not least of all at the condition of the mighty army that was gathering! Mr. Lawrence was there of course, a wonderful faithful saint for many years, he was very old, deaf and almost blind. Often, as he was not so aware of what was going on around him, Mr Lawrence would burst out in prayer at inappropriate moments or forget to stop praying when he had more than covered every topic. There was also a dear lady with a guitar who, to be honest, wasn't very good but was very willing. She would start a chorus, (that is what we called songs that were not hymns in those days), with an unidentifiable tune. We called it 'Guess a tune with Joan' and we never knew what the chorus was until we were at least half way through. In addition there were about 20 other precious saints, including children and our pastor, - a small skinny man with an abrupt, unfortunate disposition who was passionate for revival and led from the front with his big, black bible aloft.

Now to put this into context, I considered myself really rather cool! I had long hair, sharp clothes, a motorbike and use of a smart car. I had hung out with some of the 'tough guys' and together we had frequented the clubs and pubs, so to some degree I was known around town. Now however I found myself in the midst of, well, I am not sure how best to put it, maybe not such a cool crowd of people? I think this particular day generated more prayer than any other time in my life!

So, there we were about to leave the church. My prayer: "Dear God, please let it rain so this can be called off." Pastor's prayer: "Rend the heavens and let your glory pour out upon us as we reach the lost in this city through our witness." And then we were off, marching two by two down the road towards the town centre. I held my position at the back, much to the annoyance of the pastor who wanted me more visible at the front of the pack. Then the cry from the pastor went up - "Give me a J!" To which the mighty army responded with a loud shout - "J!". He continued... "Give me an E!". Again the line of elderly, precious, dysfunctional, brave, church replied - "E!" I was cringing, holding up the rear, my prayer became "Dear Jesus, if ever there was a good time for the rapture, surely it is now!'" And so the letters of the name of Jesus were duly spelled out with shouts and then rounded up by pastor with - "And what have we got?" To which the church replied - "Jesus!" Pastor was enjoying himself, the others were bewildered and I wanted the ground to swallow me up. As for those watching, well, to my relief, the streets were fairly empty but I was informed that the word of the Lord would not return to Him void but would accomplish the purpose for which it was sent, and so we marched on.

We then turned into a road heading towards the train station that was very busy and, to my horror, played host to the 'Cherry Orchard', one of the pubs I frequented with many of my old mates. "Dear God, please don't let pastor lead us up Cherry Orchard road", I pleaded. As we turned into Cherry Orchard road I continued, "Okay, I know this is a test of my faith Lord, I implore you that no one inside the pub hears what is going on outside. I bind their ears in Jesus' name!" As we approached the pub with cries of "Give me a J..." I prayed again. "Okay God, if it is really necessary to pass this place then at least don't let my old mates be in there, especially not the McCloud brothers..." (The McClouds were two of the hardest drinking, toughest fighting mates I had known and were renowned for their powers to ridicule). To my horror, as we drew adjacent to the pub the door swung open. Pastor thought the glory of God would shine into the place through the open door but instead my old mates fell out onto the pavement with the McCloud brothers at the rear! They stood, at first laughing loudly and pointing at the sight of this strange group of shouting people who had disturbed their afternoon drinking session, but when they spotted me in their vision they stared in absolute silence, eyes wide open, drinks in hand, fixated on what they saw. I looked back at them and with a shy and timid voice said - "Give me a J?" We proceeded on towards the train station accompanied by the mocking sounds of utter disbelief and amusement from the mates I once knew. I never saw them again.

I wish I could say that this experience had cured me, but I'm afraid my zeal only developed further. However I did drop the processional band idea for a then more modern witnessing attempt using technology. I created a mobile PA rig made from the frame of an old shopping trolley, a car battery and an amplifier with a cheap handheld microphone. I used to take it to the huge open-air bus station at Catford in South London at rush hour when the bus stops were full of busy commuters trying to get home, a captive audience! I set up the mobile PA rig and preached at the people. They had nowhere to go so they had to listen to my cries about the end being near, how they were destined for hell and needed to repent etc. I once had a wrestling match with a drunk who wanted to play 'The Old Rugged Cross' on his harmonica down my microphone, I won the fight but he still insisted on playing right next to me while I was preaching, leaning in so the microphone would pick him up! As I moved so did he. I pressed on regardless with pastor's voice ringing in my head, reminding me that the word of the Lord would not return unto him void etc. Eventually the Old Rugged Cross turned into an Elvis song and the crowd joined in with his rendition. I was left to pack up and head home, somewhat defeated, thinking that there had to be a better way than this!

Oh God, I am so sorry for all those I put off knowing you by my aggressive, insensitive and intrusive approach. But that was how I was taught and that was what being a disciple meant to us in the tradition of that church. I have since learned a far better and more fruitful way. Thank God.

* * *

The other area of emphasis in many circles is 'church growth'. There are now many resources available to promote and educate the church on how to pioneer and plant new works. We have many models to choose from that are often copied and implemented in the hope of multiplying the number of our churches or growing the size of our congregation. Much energy is given to this and a lot of commercial, business and marketing skills are employed to realise this objective. There is of course nothing wrong with leaders desiring growth or using our intelligence to expand what God has given us to steward. After all there is a requirement for seeing fruitfulness in that which has been entrusted to us (Gen 1:28, Matt 25:14-30). I have planted a number of churches and have always sought to see them grow so I am obviously in favour of what we understand as church growth.

There is a danger, however, that if our emphasis is primarily on growth and multiplication as our main measure of success, we have the potential of seeing the church differently to how God sees it. Each approach will produce a different set of priorities, and what we value will influence how we prioritise and spend our time, attention, money and commitment.

The head offices of various religious organisations through which we operate usually require us to provide regular statistical feedback. These relate to and reveal how well we are perceived to be doing, usually focussing on finance and numbers of attendees as a guide to success. Consequently, church leaders often find themselves under a pressure to perform and a need to be seen to be successful based on these metrics. However, not many church leaders are gifted or trained in either financial management or in marketing, nor is this likely to be the reason they first entered the ministry. Soon, however, these things become a demand on their time and attention. Now, I'm not saying that financial growth or numerical increase is bad whatsoever. Moreover. I'm sure that all movements set up to serve God have a passion for the lost and value each soul saved as treasure. What I am saying is that it is difficult to measure a 'successful' church this way. Business-like metrics do not do a particularly good job of measuring fruitfulness according to kingdom values.

Jesus has called us to be fruitful and this fruit is to be offered unto Him. It is the fruit He produces within the Church that is of the most value and it is this fruit that is priority to Him. Consequently, much of the fruit that He requires may not fit in at all with the criteria we have placed upon ourselves to measure success.

It is not easy to measure the comfort offered to the downcast, the strength given to the suffering, the marriage that is saved, the child that receives safety and encouragement, the fearful teen who finds peace, the single parent struggling alone who has been given time, advice and support. How do we measure fun? How do we measure the value of meaningful community? More importantly, how do we measure the value of worship unto God, the effectiveness of faithful prayer and the healings that take place in the body and in the soul? All of this and more is fruit that delights the Father, along with the expansion of His family, adding new people into His Kingdom and grafting them into communities. How often in our Christian communities do we ever ask if God is pleased with what we are doing or what His priority is for right now.

It doesn't take long to create a culture that is rooted in tradition. Culture is simply the way that we do things, and this is expressed in all Christian communities and movements. We value what God has said historically and what He has done in and through that movement. The tendency is to maintain momentum by continuing to operate using the same model in the same way that it has always been done. However, the Church, if it is a living, dynamic organism, is designed for change and adaptation. It is important to remember that we build not just on what God has already said but also on what God is saying today! This requires great sensitivity to Holy Spirit and clear and accurate prophetic insights that transcend and transform repetitive religious routines. Furthermore, if this is the case, then it will be essential to understand and apply how the five-fold ministry gifts to the church (Eph 4:11-13) operate, in reality, under the anointing of the Holy Spirit.

As stated previously, the word 'Church' (*'ecclesia'*) means 'called out ones' or 'assembly.' The Church is not a building erected for public worship or an organisation that runs religious activities, rather it is a living organism comprised of all those who are called by God to be worshippers and followers of Jesus Christ. The term 'called out' signifies a separation of the value system and practices of the world from higher, Kingdom values and practices. Those who have separated themselves come together to form a new assembly, the Church.

No matter how the expression manifests itself, people who gather in communities to love God, discover His ways and serve Him according to their unique set of gifts and abilities are in themselves valued by God. This is Church, alive, active and dynamic.

Jesus said that He would build His Church and the gates of hell would not prevail against it. This gives us hope and confidence that the prime responsibility for building the Church rests on God's shoulders. Before He returns as the Bridegroom He is working mysteriously with us, through us, and often despite us, to prepare the Church as a glorious Bride.

The Body of Christ

The bible refers to the Church as both the 'Body of Christ' and the 'Bride of Christ'. They are, of course, one and the same thing - the Church. Yet the body and the bride possess uniquely different functions and purposes.

The Body of Christ is a metaphor for the Church (Rom 12:5, 1 Cor 10:17; 12:27, Eph 4:12). When Jesus the Christ entered this world, He took on the form of a physical human body, not only to fully identify with humanity in every aspect but also to demonstrate the likeness, love and power of Father God in a tangible, practical and clear way. As the writer to the Hebrews puts it:

"The *Son is the radiance of God's glory and the exact representation of His being...*" (Heb 1:3)

The apostle Paul affirms this, further, revealing that :

"*He is the image of the invisible God...*" (Col 1:15)

Jesus Himself said that He only ever did what He saw His Father doing and said only what He heard His Father saying (John 5:19; 8:28).

When Jesus lived as a man on this earth He was the voice of God, the hands of God and the physical presence of God in the world. He revealed the nature, truth and ways of Father God. Jesus gave a powerful revelation of Himself and a clear indication of what He was calling His disciples to be and do when He said:

"*Don't you believe that I am in the Father, and that the Father is in me? The words I say to you I do not speak on my own authority. Rather, it is the Father, living in me, who is doing his work. Believe me when I say that I am in the Father and the Father is in me; or at least believe on the evidence of the works themselves. Very truly I tell you, whoever believes in me will do the works I have been doing, and they will do even greater things than these, because I am going to the Father. And I will do whatever you ask in my name, so that the Father may be glorified in the Son. You may ask me for anything in my name, and I will do it".* (John 14:10-14)

Here, Jesus reveals that the Father is living in Him, that He is the embodiment of the Divine and that it is the Father who has been working in and through Him. Jesus then goes on to reveal that He is going back to the Father and that they, His disciples, were to continue the work that He had started. This would be achieved by His personal presence within them. In effect they would become His body on earth in the same way that He, during His time on earth, was the body through which the Father operated. Jesus said to His Father:

"As you have sent me into the world, I have sent them into the world". (John 17:18)

Again, Jesus, in His great intercessory prayer to His Father, clearly shows that the Divine intent was to reside within the body of believers that follow Jesus, whilst simultaneously manifesting His own glory and doing His own work through them:

"My prayer is not for them alone. I pray also for those who will believe in me through their message, that all of them may be one, Father, just as you are in me and I am in you. May they also be in us so that the world may believe that you have sent me. I have given them the glory that you gave me, that they may be one as we are one - I in them and you in me - so that they may be brought to complete unity. Then the world will know that you sent me and have loved them even as you have loved me. Father, I want those you have given me to be with me where I am, and to see my glory, the glory you have given me because you loved me before the creation of the world. Righteous Father, though the world does not know you, I know you, and they

know that you have sent me. I have made you known to them, and will continue to make you known in order that the love you have for me may be in them and that I myself may be in them." (John 17:20-25)

Therefore the Body of Christ represents, literally it 're-presents', God here on earth, as ambassadors, as a royal priesthood. As a priesthood the Body interfaces with the world and with heaven, representing man before God in an intercessory way, and representing God to man both as a witness and in a ministerial sense. The Body of Christ becomes the face of God to mankind, modelling community, upholding righteousness and integrity and expressing mercy. At times the Church is called to be a prophetic voice, revealing the nature and heartbeat of God, resisting evil and speaking out for righteousness and justice. At other times the Body becomes the hands of God showing His mercy, grace and compassion through acts of kindness and generosity. The Body advances the Kingdom of God as the feet of God . It carries His Presence, truth and action through mission. The Body ministers by connecting heaven to earth through miraculous and practical means, bringing healing, deliverance, preaching and transformation. The Body manifests the Presence of God, changes atmospheres and is often the means of holding back evil.

The Body of Christ is far more than just a discipleship factory or an expanding religious business. Winning the lost to Christ is essential and seeking to grow is commendable, but that is not all that the Church is about. Being the Body of Christ includes that but it is in fact far more. This is made even more evident when we consider the Church as the Bride of Christ.

The Bride of Christ

Whilst the Body of Christ is the functioning community of Jesus' followers, serving the world on behalf of God, the Bride of Christ has little to do with ministering to mankind. The Bride is that which is created by God wholly and solely for Himself, the entire redeemed community is being prepared for the Bridegroom. The prime concern for the Bride is Her relationship with God. It is about love, devotion, intimacy and a passion for His presence. The Bride is designed to produce fruit that is entirely for God, that which pleases Him alone. As the Bride, the Church yields the fruit of love, integrity, righteousness, holiness, sacrifice, peace, endurance and the like (Gal 5:22-23). This fruit of the Spirit is the expression of a quality of character flowing out of a nature that reveals and reflects the Divine.

The Bride, through Her worship, mirrors back to God who He is, what He is like, what He has done through creation, redemption, sustaining life etc. The Bride adores the Bridegroom by offering praise, declaring His greatness, acknowledging His goodness and expressing thanksgiving.

The Bride passionately loves the Bridegroom and dwells in His presence, communing with Him, experiencing and seeking to serve Him, ministering to His desires. It is a role of submission, devotion, adoration and unrelenting intimacy.

Scripture reveals that the Bride is being prepared for the return of the Bridegroom, The Church is being made ready for His eternal and glorious purposes:

"Let us rejoice and be glad and give him glory! For the wedding of the Lamb has come, and his bride has made herself ready. Fine linen, bright and clean, was given her to wear." (Rev 19:7-8)

"I saw the Holy City, the new Jerusalem, coming down out of heaven from God, prepared as a bride beautifully dressed for her husband." (Rev 21:2)

"The Spirit and the bride say, 'Come!' And let the one who hears say, 'Come!' Let the one who is thirsty come; and let the one who wishes take the free gift of the water of life." (Rev 22:17)

I feel that there is a greater emphasis here regarding the work of Divine grace in realising the dream of God, rather than focussing on the efforts of man to manufacture and maintain an organisation. Emphasising the dream of God causes some of our priorities, which can be so wrapped up in trivia, politics, preference and ambitions, to pale into insignificance. Perhaps this small book may reveal a glimpse into what the priority of God is for His Church at this time.

When we are in line with God's prophetic agenda this invariably produces fruit and achieves His purposes. Although this may not be in agreement with much of the Church's current preferences, values and priorities, it is worth checking to be sure that we are on the same wavelength as Holy Spirit.

Back in the summer of 2018 I was going to begin a series called 'Hosting His Presence' in our then home church in St Albans. The goal was to keep in line with what God had been speaking to us about, - preparing for His Presence and preparing for harvest. I asked for a model of the Ark of the Covenant to be built and placed inside a structure covered in drapes to represent the Tabernacle of David. This would be a visual illustration of that which I was about to teach and I was excited to unpack the huge significance of the rebuilding of the tabernacle of David (Acts 15, Amos 9) in our day and in our time. I feel that we are in days when God is inspiring 'Davids' to rise up and bring the Presence of God back into the house of God.

The life sized model of the Tabernacle of David and the Ark were duly constructed and placed in a corner of our church ready for meetings the following day. When the team arrived to set up on Sunday morning they found the 'Tabernacle' broken, twisted and lying in a heap on top of the Ark. No one had been in the building and there was no wind or any logical explanation for this. Everyone was bewildered, especially as some force would have been needed not only to break the retaining joints of the construction but also to lift and rotate it 180 degrees to its final collapsed position. We cleared away the wreckage and postponed the series.

In February 2019 we decided to recreate the model and teach the 'Hosting His Presence' series which we had previously cancelled. One of our team was adding final touches to the angels mounted on the top of the Ark. He went to the store cupboard to get some tools and upon his return he discovered the whole thing had collapsed in exactly the same way as before! Once again everything was in a pile on top of the Ark. My first thought was that this was the devil's work, trying to stop the revelation of the glory of God in the midst of His people. We should pray through the place and continue on regardless! However, my son Joshua felt that maybe God was communicating something different, about how His glory can no longer be contained in a man-made structure. Alternatively, He is destroying old structures to reveal His glory. Either way it did seem to be a strange, supernatural occurrence, so we continued to pray and seek God's wisdom on these unusual events.

I communicated with a number of my prophetic friends, seeking their insight into what had happened. The general thinking was that God would not be contained in a box, that the collapsed Tabernacle reflected much of the church in this season, not valuing Presence and too caught up in its own busyness and activity, about to collapse. Ichabod is the name over many churches nowadays and God is about to destroy man-made structures that try to shroud rather than reveal His glory.

I would suggest that the vast majority of modern churches energy, focus and activities are primarily about the satisfaction of man. We tend to look at church from our own perspective, wanting it to meet our requirements and preferences rather than viewing it from a Divine perspective, as God sees and values it. He is shaking so much of what we have held dear but no longer has a place in what He is building to reveal His true glory.

God is rebuilding the fallen tabernacle of David in our day, just as He did through Paul, James, Peter and others, blowing their minds as Holy Spirit revealed a plan and purpose for the 'called out ones' that was way beyond their initial grasp or expectations. They had to come to terms with the fact that God was expressing grace and moving outside of the established religious model, drawing gentiles into faith in Him whilst expressing huge grace and favour upon them. As good Jews who had rightly understood that they were God's chosen people and that through them He would bring salvation to the world, or at least reveal God to the world, this was difficult for them to accept. However, they could not deny what God was obviously doing, something completely new. He was raising up a new body that was neither Jewish nor gentile, but one body comprising of all those who have faith in Christ.

This new body are the true children of Abraham on account of the faith that God had given to them (Gal 3:6-9). This new 'temple' was now created to be a holy temple, the dwelling place of God on earth, the house of the Divine (Eph 2:19-22). This new dwelling place was not to be made of bricks or stone like a physical building, but rather out of living stones; you and I, redeemed humans who are formed into a holy priesthood. The design and intent of God is that we offer spiritual sacrifices that are acceptable to Him, the Father (1 Peter 2:4-5). That looks quite different to what most of us have become accustomed to in church world over the years! A living organism, not an organisation. A dynamic body created by God, comprised of redeemed humans who are filled with Divine Presence, each part expressing the uniqueness of their personality, ability, character and role, and primarily expressed God-ward not man-ward. Holy Spirit is committed to preparing and rebuilding this unique expression of the Church. He is preparing His Bride for the return of the King.

ESTHER – PREPARATION FOR PURPOSE

The story of Esther was written around the fourth century before Christ and is about God's providential care of His people. Although the name of God is not mentioned within the book, He is alluded to throughout it. Esther was a Jewish maiden who became Queen of Persia and was used to deliver her people from a massacre. The King of Persia, Xerxes, ruled over the known world at that time and His kingdom extended from India to Egypt and was divided into 127 provinces. Today it is hard for us to grasp just how powerful kings were in the ancient world. They ruled with absolute authority and their command was to be obeyed at all costs. Xerxes, like all conquering kings, was a warlord to be feared. Yet within his realm security, provision and prosperity could be found, subject to loyalty and obedience.

In the third year of his reign Xerxes gave a banquet for all of his nobles, officials, military leaders and heads of provinces. This was a grand affair and for 180 days he displayed the vast wealth of his kingdom. After this was over a 7 day banquet began in the enclosed gardens of the king's palace. This banquet was open to all the people who lived in the citadel of Susa, from the least to the greatest. Elaborate decorations festooned the garden, with hangings of white and blue linen fastened to silver rings on marble pillars by cords of white and purple. The couches on which they sat were gold and silver. There was a mosaic pavement of marble, mother of pearl and other costly stones. The wine was served in golden goblets, each one different from the next, and there was an abundance of royal wine, in keeping with the king's liberality. He allowed each person to drink as much as they wanted and by and large it was a great time. Although Xerxes was not a worshipper of Yahweh, I feel this event portrays something of a picture of heaven with the great banquet celebrating the King, - an extravagance of decoration, food and wine.

However, we read in the book of Esther that on the last day of the banquet the king invited his queen, Vashti, to come and display her beauty to his guests. She refused and instead she held her own party, - probably not too surprising considering that their marriage was not really a match made in heaven! Vashti was a Babylonian princess, the granddaughter of Nebuchadnezzar and daughter of Belshazar. Her royal lineage and pedigree were immaculate, she was a chosen and privileged daughter of the Babylonian royal household. However, Darius the Persian king invaded Babylon, kidnapped Vashti, killed her father Belshazar and gave her as a bride to his son Xerxes.

Her refusal to obey Xerxes and insistence on fulfilling her own agenda was a dangerous choice. This obviously humiliated and annoyed the king so he sought advice from his counsellors, who in turn suggested that her behaviour might send the wrong signal to other women in the country who may also become rebellious. The king's advisors therefore counselled him to be rid of Vashti and find another queen, and Xerxes agreed. After some time the king's personal attendants proposed that a search be made for a beautiful young virgin for the king, and this is where Esther comes into the story.

Esther was an orphan that had been raised by her older cousin, Mordecai. They had been among the Jews taken into exile from Jerusalem to Babylon by King Nebuchadnezzar. This meant that she had no parents and was taken first to Babylon, a long way from her national home. She was an exile in every sense. Once the Persians conquered the Babylonians she, along with many others, was then taken into deeper captivity even further from her homeland and all that she knew as familiar. Orphaned, exiled, captive! A young girl left to fend for herself in an alien land and locked into servitude. Thank God for Mordecai who took her in and raised her.

Esther did have some natural, God-given advantages, - she was very lovely in both form and features. Once the king's edict had been proclaimed, many girls were brought to the citadel of Susa and put under the care of Hegai, the master of the harem. Esther was one of these girls and because she pleased Hegai and won his favour he rewarded her with beauty treatments, special foods and the services of seven maids.

It is worth noting that Hegai was a eunuch which means that he was emasculated. The idea behind this was that he would be dedicated to preparing the bride for the king, but he would have no personal desire for her himself. I believe this is a prophetic metaphor for leaders in the Church today, God is raising up 'eunuchs' to lead His people and prepare them as a bride for the king. A contrast to those who see God's people as a means to their own end, using the Bride of Christ, the Church, to build their name, reputation or empire, often under the guise of their ministry. "Eunuch" leaders have only one desire and that is to serve the king. They live to enable His Bride to be prepared wholly unto Him.

The other side of this part of the story is that Esther found favour with Hegai and he helped her to negotiate the precarious path of being transformed from a pauper, an orphan, an exile, without any idea of how to behave in a royal court, unaware of the protocols but seemingly willing to learn, into a prospective queen. In fact the secret of her success was in her obedience to Hegai. Her cooperation and demonstration of right attitude towards her development made it easy for Hegai to show her favour. I'm sure any leader would agree that favour is more likely to be shown to those who display cooperation, servant heartedness and obedience rather than to someone who is awkward, complaining and contentious!

We read that the king was very attracted to Esther and she won his favour and approval more than any other virgin, so he set his royal crown on her head and made her queen instead of Vashti. The king then gave a great banquet for all of his nobles and officials and proclaimed a holiday throughout the province, distributing gifts with royal liberality.

What can we discover from this story? First of all we learn that the king was extravagant, liberal, generous and wanted to share the riches of his kingdom with his subjects. Secondly, we see that although queen Vashti was invited to join him in the celebrations, to display her beauty to everyone gathered there, she refused and instead held her own party.

This reminds me of the story Jesus told in Luke 14:16 and Matthew 22:1-14, of the king who had prepared a wedding banquet for his son. He sent his servants out to those who had already been invited, telling them to come quickly as the preparations were complete. Unfortunately those guests had found other things to occupy their time. One said that he had just bought a field and must attend to it; another had bought five yoke of oxen and had to try them out; another had just got married and it appeared that his wife wouldn't let him come. The servants returned to the king and informed him of their responses. The king ordered the servants to go out again, into the streets and alleys of the town and bring in the poor, the crippled, the blind and the lame, - all the people who thought they would never receive an invitation from a king. They were outcasts, the rejects of society, non-religious, unworthy, and yet the king preferred to have them rather than those were previously invited but rejected his invitation.

Following the response of the outcasts there was still room at the wedding feast, so the king then told his servants to go into the roads and country lanes and compel people to come in so that his house might be full. The king was throwing a wide net and drawing in anyone who was willing to accept his free offer, - after all, the hungry and the thirsty will always go where there is food and drink. The self-satisfied, preoccupied and self-sufficient prefer to carry on doing their own thing rather than enter into the will and desire of the king. So it was with Vashti, who preferred to hold a party with her own friends rather than respond in obedience to the king and enter into his celebration.

I am reminded too of Luke 15:11-31 when the brother of the lost son refused to enter into his father's celebration following the return home of his younger son. He was offended and thought the younger brother was unworthy, so refused to associate with him. In his own self-righteousness he remained outside the celebrations, refusing to share in his father's joy. We must note however, that in both Jesus' account of the king's banquet and the story of Vashti, the king rejected those who refused his invitation and instead searched for guests who would respond to him in the right way.

Responding correctly to one another is essential for healthy relationships. It is only those who have an intimate relationship with a family or friend who normally get an invitation to a wedding and its subsequent celebration. We read in Revelation 19:

"Blessed are those who are invited to the wedding supper of the Lamb."

This implies an existing intimacy and sign of friendship. We would only want those who are our friends and family to be at our wedding. It is often deemed an insult to refuse the honour but counted a privilege to receive such an invitation.

When our eldest daughter Laura was planning her wedding I was initially horrified at the number of guests she wanted. It looked as though everyone she had ever met while backpacking around Europe and Asia was on the invitation list. Fortunately, distance proved a problem so we ended up with a more reasonable number, - I guess most dads would identify with that particular challenge! I knew that I was in for a rough ride when, during the initial planning stages of the wedding, I spoke with my wife and daughter in a fatherly, firm, yet generous way and suggested what their budget would be. They together instantaneously burst into laughter, looked at each other and laughed again. My wife lovingly told me it would be at least double that and that Laura and her husband to be would also be contributing. I withdrew gracefully and began to increase my prayer time.

PREPARING
THE BRIDE

Returning to Esther's story, we notice that some rejected and some accepted the king's invitation to enter into his blessing and take part in the banquet. For those who accepted the invitation, like Esther, there was a period of preparation before presentation to the king. It took Esther twelve months of beauty treatments, six months of oil and myrrh and six months of perfumes and cosmetics.

This is the challenge for us today. Holy Spirit is preparing the Bride of Christ for the return of the Bridegroom, King Jesus. Now this concept is a challenge for the task orientated and project needy among us. It would appear that there is a different priority in the heart of God to that of our own! If God is calling us to enter into a season of preparation, oil, perfume, myrrh and cosmetics, there is a fair chance most of us don't want to sign up for that. We would prefer power, action, achievement and victories. There is nothing wrong with that in and of itself, however we don't see Jesus driven with endless activity. What we do see is a model of Him responding to the leading of His Father in heaven, which produced fruit, fruit that will last. Our tendency is to engage in endless busy-ness, resulting in little fruit. I believe God is trying to capture our attention, not to be disengaged in evangelism or Holy Spirit led initiatives, but to respond to what He is doing in preparing the Bride for the Bridegroom. This is not an outward focus on attainment but an internal transformation that will cause our ministries to be far more fruitful than we have ever known.

"Those who know their God will be strong and carry out great exploits" (Dan 11:32).

Preparation with oil

We know that oil is symbolic of the Holy Spirit. It speaks of the priestly anointing and being soaked in the anointing power of the Holy Spirit. There is a need for us to know, experience Holy Spirit, to allow Him to soak us in His divine presence and be loved by Him just for the sake of being loved. To become so impregnated with His presence that we "know" Him, His voice, His feelings, His vision and aspirations. In reality, how much time do we spend communing alone with God? From the Desert Fathers to the Celtic monastics and other movements of God people have sought to separate themselves out from the world to engage personally with Him. They sought time and space to be in His presence, engage Spirit to spirit, and in turn their ministry became God filled and fruitful.

God longs for you to waste time with Him, alone. Not to seek Him for power, vision or provision, but for who He is and to know Him as He is, not as we have created Him to be. We need to be in that secret place with the Most High, allowing Him to fill us, impress the weight of His presence upon us and leave His hallmark. This is life transforming time, learning to hear His voice in silence, allowing Him to massage us with the oil of His anointed presence, softening our hearts and easing the stiffness and resistance of our will to His, ruined by His love and grace, soaked in rest and peace of soul. This can only truly be found in solitude, alone with God.

I believe this is why the first apostles told the Church they could not be given to waiting on tables, caught up in the distraction of administrative things, rather they had to give themselves to prayer and the ministry of God's word (Acts 6:1-4). The result of prioritising time with God is evident in the book of Acts where we are told that many came to faith in Christ through their preaching, miracles occurred and transformation took place.

Henry Nouwen, in his classic book 'The Way Of The Heart', explores the spirituality of the Desert Fathers and Mothers. He advocates three ways to stop the world influencing and shaping us into its mould. These same three ways promote life in the Spirit. The first being 'solitude,' the second being 'silence' and the third being 'praying always'. I highly recommend this book to anyone serious about their spirituality and I am confident that every leader who reads it will be deeply affected by its message. It has the potential to springboard you into a new sphere of engagement with God.

Years ago, I went up to Scotland to see an old friend, Hugh Black. He had been used by God extensively in healing and deliverance and carried with him passion and energy for revival. It was just a week or so before he went home to be with Jesus and I asked him for a father's blessing. While fixing his eyes deep into mine he told me that I already had the Father's blessing but went on to say, "If you want to know true anointing then lock yourself up alone with God, listen to His voice and do what He says."

His words made a lasting impact. The highlight of my day is usually first thing in the morning, when I shut myself away in silence, communing with God's divine presence before I proceed into my work of prayer, study and ministry.

Processed with myrrh

Myrrh has two symbolic implications; Firstly, it was one of three ingredients used in the holy anointing oil which was poured onto the high priest's robes. Oil was mixed with aloes, cassia and myrrh. When this mixture when placed onto the priest's garment it gave off a sweet fragrance and it was often possible to smell the priest coming before you could see him. Some have even noticed a beautiful fragrance when the anointed presence of the Lord Jesus surrounds them. This speaks of the priestly role of the Church as we stand between God and man, interceding for the world.

I recall times in our worship when people have noticed a sweet, spicy smell waft around the room, sometimes lingering in locations or over people. I believe this to be the manifest presence of Jesus in our midst, the anointing oil upon His high priestly robes, impregnated with aloes, cassia and myrrh, being released into the atmosphere and assuring us of His divine presence and approval. God desires to release His presence among His people, to impress Himself upon us experientially so that we begin to bear the presence of God, change atmospheres and bring influence wherever God has placed us.

The second symbolic representation of myrrh is that of death. It was used in the preparation of bodies for burial and can therefore speak of death to our flesh life. It is true to say that we will never truly know resurrection life until there has been a death and Jesus spoke about this extensively;

"For whoever wants to save their life will lose it, but whoever loses their life for me and for the gospel will save it." (Mark 8:35)

Jesus is speaking here about the priorities of living for Him over and above our own ambitions and desires.

'Then Jesus said to his disciples, "Whoever wants to be my disciple must deny themselves and take up their cross and follow me."'(Matt 16:24)

A cross can represent a place of execution or a burden to bear. Here, Jesus once again emphasises that true discipleship necessitates dying to oneself and living with self-denial in order to realise the higher purpose of the kingdom of God. This is a deep work of the Holy Spirit influencing our lives, transforming us into true sons of the Father; a process where our love for the sinful things of this world pales into insignificance in the light of His glory and grace. Our ambitions and motives change, we are not what we once were. The old way of life drops off and we are transformed into what Father designed and destined us to be. This continues as we learn to make decisions based on living primarily for God rather than satisfying our old nature with its sinful habits and motives.

The apostle Paul said:

"So then, death is at work in us, but life is at work in you". (2 Cor 4:12)

And towards the end of his life he reflected:

"For I am already being poured out like a drink offering, and the time for my departure is near". (2 Tim 4:6)

Paul lived a lifetime of giving himself relentlessly to the advancement of the cause of Christ and looking forward to entering into heaven to receive his just reward.

While it may seem glum to think God requires us to die, the notion behind it is that we lose our husk, our outer shell of protection, so that the true kernel of who we are in Christ might be released and we may bear fruit. It is an ongoing process of laying down our lives so that the life of Christ might be seen in us and we bear fruit that will last.

There seems to be no other way into the abundant life that Jesus speaks of, nor alternative way of experiencing the true power of the Spirit, without first crucifying our flesh. 'Flesh' includes ambition, pride, ego and self-righteousness. John the Baptist declared that Christ must increase and that he, John, must decrease. All too often people want power for their ministry, finance or projects, all in the name of Jesus, but is it really for Jesus or is it for their own ambitious vision? We are forever seeking the hand of God but failing to seek His face, rarely seeking Him for who He is but rather for what we can get from Him.

God is putting to death works that only amount to wood, hay and stubble, works not borne in the heart of God, but rather in the heart of proud and ambitious men and women using the name of God for their own ends. The Holy Spirit is working death in our flesh lives so that the life of the Spirit may have great prominence. There is only one way to resurrection life and it is the way of the cross. Every other way is a deception!

Preparation with Cosmetics

After being soaked in oil and myrrh for six months, Esther undertook another six months of preparatory treatment with perfumes and cosmetics. Now, my wife used to be a beauty therapist and over the years I have gained some insights into the use of cosmetics! What I have discovered is that cosmetics can enhance and highlight our good features and camouflage blemishes that we may want to hide.

When some ladies go out for an evening or attend a special occasion they may enjoy spending time getting ready and this often involves cosmetics. Through creativity and skilful application of make up they can reveal and highlight a natural God given beauty, make a statement, express fun, personality and even add some glamour! They may also choose to cover blemishes or scars. For some individuals this may be important for their self-confidence, to minimise that which they prefer to conceal.

To this end I can see the work of the Holy Spirit in our lives, preparing us as the Bride of Christ, soaking us in His presence and drawing from us our true personalities in all their beauty and uniqueness. Those areas of our lives that are ugly due to sin and damage are covered with the blood of Jesus, bringing cleansing and healing to our hurts, wounds and blemishes with His grace and mercy. Instead of exaggerating our damage it is camouflaged until the recovery process has been completed and it can be included in the whole perfected picture. Then the 'cosmetics' of God can highlight our healed and whole personality to glorify Him and display His work of grace, love and restoration.

A beautiful illustration of this can be found in the story of King David and Mephibosheth (2 Sam 4:4; 9). David, now established on the throne, inquired as to who was left of the former King Saul's family. The normal procedure in these circumstances would be to kill all the remaining members of the old dynasty in order to eliminate any threat to your own throne. It was revealed to King David that the grandson of Saul, Mephibosheth, was still alive. Now Mephibosheth was disabled. In a moment of panic in the kings palace he had been dropped by his nurse whilst trying to flee from danger and he remained damaged all of his life. King David summoned him into his presence and when Mephibosheth entered he said; "What is your servant, that you should notice a dead dog like me?" Now there is someone in need of healing, both physically for his damaged legs, but also emotionally for a self-image that identified with that of a dead dog! However, David says "Don't be afraid, ... I will show you kindness, ... you will always eat at my table." So, Mephibosheth ate at the King's table. When he entered into the royal household, by royal decree, he slid his damaged legs under the table and sat with dignity and full rights, equal to any of the King's sons. His damaged hidden, unobservable, his true royal destiny revealed. That is what God does in our lives. He takes that which is broken, ashamed and damaged, and through His grace allows us, with full authority, to sit at the king's table, our stigma covered, head held high because of royal acceptance, royal choosing and royal decree. No one dare to contradict the King's instructions and wishes. This is divine cosmetics in action!

Preparation with Perfumes

The perfumes used in preparing Esther are highly significant. Once perfumes are applied they release a unique fragrance on the wearer and that fragrance can change the surrounding atmosphere.

Paul gives an illustration of us being the fragrance of Christ:

"But thanks be to God, who always leads us as captives in Christ's triumphal procession and uses us to spread the aroma of the knowledge of Him everywhere. For we are to God the pleasing aroma of Christ among those who are being saved and those who are perishing. To the one we are an aroma that brings death; to the other, an aroma that brings life. And who is equal to such a task?" (2 Cor 2:14-16)

This fragrance is the aroma of the knowledge of God and the aroma of Christ everywhere to everyone. I believe the idea behind Pauls revelation is that of a Roman army returning to its garrison town after a victorious battle. As the army entered the town in glory following their great victory, the women and children would not only line the streets applauding them but would also throw flower petals in front of the marching soldiers. As they marched over the petals they crushed them underfoot releasing a sweet fragrance into the atmosphere. To them this was the sweet smell of victory. However, it was the smell of defeat to those who were being dragged along in chains at the rear of the procession. They were now slaves of their conquerers. To one the smell of victory, to the other, although the same sweet smell, it was the fragrance of defeat.

So it is with us, as we bear the presence of Christ we become the sweet smell of heaven, revealing the knowledge and presence of Christ. We bring hope, we change atmospheres, we are the means God uses to transform lives. However, to those who hate God, who rebel against Him and His ways, who choose to follow anything other than Christ, who remain bound in their sin and suffering its consequences, to them this is the smell of defeat.

Jesus, our high priest who carries the fragrance of heaven, encountered both of these reactions from those who met Him. On one occasion when He was in the synagogue a demonised man cried out:

"What do you want with us Jesus of Nazareth? Have you come to destroy us? I know who you are - the Holy One of God!" (Mark 1:24)

Incredibly, the demon instantly recognised who Jesus was, the Messiah, just by being in His presence. The fragrance of Christ impregnated the atmosphere and affected all that was around. The enemy certainly knew its destiny and impending destruction. It was the smell of defeat for the unclean spirit.

Yet this same Jesus, releasing the same fragrance of His presence, signalled victory, life and hope to others. Following the healing of Peter's mother-in-law the scripture tells us that after sunset the people brought the sick and demonised to Jesus. It was as if the whole town had gathered at the door. Jesus' presence attracted all those in need and he healed them (Mark 1:32-34).

Isaiah 60 says:

"Arise shine, for your light has come, and the glory of the LORD rises upon you. See, darkness covers the earth and thick darkness is over the peoples, but the LORD rises upon you and His glory appears over you. Nations will come to the brightness of your dawn."

I am convinced that it will be the intensity of God's presence, the release of His fragrance and the manifest presence of His glory that will draw out of darkness those who are attracted to the light. But this same light will produce rage and hatred in those who are evil and choose to remain in darkness. Persecution may result because the demons hate to be reminded of their destiny and they roam like a lion seeking whom they may devour. Nonetheless, it is the fragrant presence of Christ that will inspire hope and remind us of our destiny in Him.

We can only become that fragrance by allowing God to soak us in His Spirit and impregnate our character with myrrh. Moreover, we must experience the divine as a priority in our lives and seek His manifest presence in our midst. We must allow God to heal the damaged self-image, formed through pain, wounding and the damage of our past life, knowing that we now have the right to take our rightful royal decreed place at the King's table. It takes time to soak, time worth prioritising if we are ever going to bear His presence in the market place and change atmospheres.

✳ ✳ ✳

We note that Esther was given special favour and won the approval of those attending to her before she was presented to the King. This speaks of God's grace, generosity, and the abundance of His favour towards us when we are willing to receive the ministry of God's love into our lives, - allowing Him to beautify us before we are presented to the one true King.

I believe we are entering into a time of the fulfilment of Isaiah 61:2, which says that it is now '...the year of the Lord's favour', a time when we can experience God's blessing rather than labouring under the curse of death that religion often brings. It is now time to move into the blessings of God and allow Him to minister His love and healing into our lives through intimacy. Like Esther, we may feel that we are orphans, abandoned and rejected. But the Father calls us into His palace, right up to the banqueting table, where we may know that we are loved and accepted as we are, not as we ought to be.

This whole process of being refined and knowing more of His abiding presence, which is like being soaked with His oil and myrrh or treated with perfumes and cosmetics, is all part of the preparation of the Bride. Our very personality and character becomes impregnated with Him so that His glory is manifest in our lives.

* * *

This is a process of preparation initiated by Holy Spirit to transition us from poverty to royalty in all aspects of our lives. Esther was taken as an orphan with all of her common failings, frailty and faults, rejected and living a long way from her natural home, but chosen by God for noble purpose. By His sovereign plan He transformed her from a captive pauper to a princess, to be presented to the king not as a servant but as His wife!

God has no intention of leaving us where we were found. He provides all that is necessary to cleanse, heal and restore us back to His original design, enabling us to bear the presence of the King, because we have spent time with Him and co-operated with Holy Spirit in transforming us into true sons of the Father.

THE BRIDE HAS MADE HERSELF READY

Preparation of the Bride

I remember the day Karen and I were married. I sat at the front of the church next to my brother, who was my best man, waiting for my bride to arrive. The church was full of guests who had travelled the length and breadth of the country to be with us. Excitement filled the air as we awaited her arrival. It seemed like an eternity! Karen was only twenty minutes late, but it seemed like forever to me. Suddenly the music struck up to announce her arrival and we all stood and turned to greet her. I looked and saw a vision of beauty. Everything about her made my heart swell. Her dress was magnificent, her hair perfectly arranged and make-up expertly done, enhancing the natural beauty of her face. She was my bride and I so appreciated all the effort she had put into her preparation for this day.

Had Karen arrived wearing an old pair of Levi's, tatty trainers and with food stuck between her teeth I don't think I would have been quite so impressed, nor would I have considered that the day meant anything of real importance to her. Praise God this was not the case!

As the time for the return of the Lord fast approaches there is a work that the Holy Spirit is doing in the Bride to make herself ready for her Bridegroom.

Corporate Individuality

We have to view the Church not only as a corporate body but also as a tribe of autonomous believers. In its entirety the Church is comprised of individuals, and when the Bible speaks to us corporately it also speaks to us at an individual level. It is only when we individually start to change and become renewed that together we experience renewal. The tendency is for us to talk in corporate terms, enabling us to avoid personal responsibility, always waiting for 'them' and 'those people' to get their act together.

I believe there are four major emphases which are the primary focus of Holy Spirit in preparing the Church for the return of Jesus. The first is intimacy with God and each other, the second is a call to holiness, the third is living in healing and wholeness and the fourth is equipping an end time army.

Intimacy

Part of the process of God preparing the Bride is to bring us into a new level of intimacy and relationship with the Lord Jesus. During this time of betrothal we can discover more about Him, His ways, plans and purposes, so that we too can share in His heart's desires as we grow closer to Him and become more like Him.

Jesus often made startling statements that at time brought offence to the hearers, but His words were always meant to challenge, to provoke thought and to bring about changed lives. One such occasion is found in Matthew 18, when the disciples came to Jesus asking who was to be the greatest in heaven. Jesus' response was to bring a child to stand among them, then He said:

'I tell you the truth, unless you change and become like little

children, you will never enter the kingdom of heaven. Therefore, whoever humbles himself like this child is the greatest in the kingdom of heaven.'

Three key words emerge from this passage like a light piercing the darkness. Change. Humble. Child.

First of all, we have to look at the word 'change', which in this particular context means to repent. It is like journeying along one path, changing your mind and going back the way you came. Jesus offers this challenge of repentance to us all when change is needed.

The second word to consider is 'humble'. We read in James 4:6 (quoting from Proverbs 3:34):

"God opposes the proud but gives grace to the humble."

This means that God is diametrically opposed to those who have a proud heart, no matter how right they are or how correct their theology, doctrine, practice or tradition may be. However, He gives grace to the humble, even though they may have imperfect theology, deficient practice and no tradition. This is a tremendous challenge to many of us because we have been so proud of our correctness, our accomplishments, our systems and visions. We may find that God has set His face to directly oppose us because of the issues of our hearts, while often the inefficient and less educated can be experiencing the grace and favour of God because of the condition of their humble hearts.

The third word that shines out of this passage is 'child'. We are told to humble ourselves like a child, and it seems our measure of childlikeness is linked to our stature in the kingdom of heaven. However, initially there appears to be a contradiction here, - God calls us to be mature but also childlike. Well, it may be that God is not advocating childishness in the sense of immaturity, which is unfortunately predominant in certain sections of the church, but rather *childlikeness*. A healthy child in a secure environment will be very trusting, will depend upon his or her parents, be vulnerable, playful, innocent, teachable, meek, spontaneous, impulsive and aware of what is happening around them. Maybe we have lost these childlike qualities in our walk with the Lord and have become self-dependent, self-protective, mistrusting, unteachable, proud and forgotten how to play and enjoy our Christian life. We may have lost spontaneity and impulsive responses to the things of the Spirit of God and become grown-up, controlling adults who think they know best.

The challenge Jesus brings is that unless we *change* and *become like children* again through the process of *humility* we will never enter into the things of the kingdom of heaven.

Jesus was once challenged by the religious people of His day who asked what was the greatest of all the commandments. He responded by quoting Deuteronomy 6:5:

'"Love the Lord your God with all your heart and with all your soul and with all your strength." This is the first and greatest commandment. And the second is like it: "Love your neighbour as yourself." All the law and the Prophets hang on these two commandments.'

In other words, by loving God, experiencing His love for us and loving our neighbour as we love ourselves we are fulfilling the law of God. It is as simple as that. Everything in the Christian faith hangs on this command, yet we have complicated Christian lives and allowed other issues and circumstances to cloud our vision of Jesus. This causes us to veer away from His primary objectives for our lives, - away from loving God and loving each other.

In Revelation chapter 2 we see a letter that Jesus wrote to the Ephesian church. Our Lord commends them for their perseverance, for enduring hardships, working hard, not tolerating wickedness and testing false apostles. In verse 4, however, we read:

"Yet I hold this against you: You have forsaken your first love."

Or as the New Living Translation puts it:

"You don't love me or others as you did at first."

Jesus goes on to challenge them to remember the height from which they had fallen (humble), to repent (change), and do the things they did at first (childlikeness). This solemn warning continues, saying that if they do not repent and do what they did at first then He would come and remove their 'lamp-stand from its place'. The word of God is true, and we are warned that God resists the proud but gives grace to the humble.

It may be that we, too, have lost our first love, just like the Ephesian church. We have been preoccupied with preserving truth, enduring hardships, resisting wickedness, working hard, and testing that which appears to be false within the Church. But our time may have become so absorbed by the devil and warfare that we have been chasing our tails and forsaken the most important commandment of all, to love God and allow Him to love us. Instead of us pulsating with the love and vibrancy of the Holy Spirit, many of us have become bankrupt on the inside, trying to perform to gain the approval of God and of others.

There is a desperate need for us to know the love of God in Christ Jesus again, to melt away the ice and hardness that has gripped our hearts and hinders us from hearing the things of the Spirit. Jesus challenges us to remember where we have come from and repent, humbling ourselves and becoming childlike again - spontaneous, impulsive, meek, teachable, playful, vulnerable, dependent upon Him. If we fall in love with Jesus again, He will reveal His love for us, but if we do not, the lamp-stand (presence of God) will be removed from its place.

There is a strong biblical basis for acknowledging that if we turn away from God, and fail to follow His ways, He will remove His abiding presence. Consider the tragic story of when Israel lost the Ark of the Covenant to the Philistines during the days of Eli the priest (1 Sam 4). Eli had failed to discipline his sons for their contemptible behaviour and therefore God allowed the Ark, which represented the abiding presence of God in the midst of His people, to be captured. Not only was the Ark taken by the enemy, which alone brought shame and disgrace, but the Philistines had also inflicted an enormous defeat upon the Israelites. More than 30,000 soldiers died, and the remaining men fled to their own tents. In the process Eli's two sons were killed. When Eli heard of this, he was so shocked at the news that he fell backwards off his chair, broke his neck and died. When his daughter-in-law, who was pregnant, heard that her husband and father-in-law were both dead, and that the Ark had been captured, she went into premature labour. Although she successfully gave birth to a son, she was so overcome by her labour pains that she too died. Before she passed away, she named the boy Ichabod, meaning '*no glory*', saying, "The glory of the Lord has departed from Israel."

As the presence of the Lord departs, so His protective, providing blessing goes with Him, leaving only curse and consequence to contend with. Just as Vashti and those invited to the king's banquet were rejected, it is possible that we too can be rejected because we have lost our first love. By reason of lost relationship, we also lose contact with His presence and are no longer in clear or meaningful communication. We are therefore unable to hear His voice and know His specific will, purpose or plan for us. This leads to presumption and our response is to act as we see fit or as Saul put it "I felt compelled....," but he stepped way beyond his call and anointing and thus invoked the judgement of God. Just because we "feel" or look at our circumstances as Saul did, trying to fix things in panic, doesn't mean we are responding in obedience to God or fulfilling the divine plan for our lives or those around us. Samuel told him clearly:

> "*To obey is better than sacrifice, and to heed is better than the*

fat of rams. For rebellion is like the sin of divination, and arrogance like the evil of idolatry. Because you have rejected the Lord, he has rejected you as king." (1 Sam 15:22-23)

As previously mentioned, Jesus said that unless we repent He will come and take our lamp-stand from its place. Revelation 2:7 says:

"He who has an ear, let him hear what the Spirit says to the churches."

Love is a priority for God. He desires more than anything else to love us and be loved by us in return. Very often we hold God at a distance by acknowledging His majesty, greatness and might, yet when Jesus came to earth He was known as Emmanuel, 'God with us', demonstrating His desire to be intimate and accessible, - someone with whom we can build relationship. We know too that Jesus always worked *with* God rather than *for* God. We see in John 5:19 that Jesus only did what He saw the Father doing and in John 12:49 we read that Jesus only said what He heard the Father saying.

At all times it appears that Jesus operated from a position of rest. Psalm 46:10 says:

"Be still and know that I am God."

In our modern world of activity and pressure we find it so difficult just to be still and know Him. To know Him in intimacy and give time to renew that relationship is essential. Ephesians 3:17-21 tells us that we are rooted and established in love. God is love. We have a theology of it, but very often we have little experience of it. Christ, the Bridegroom, is coming for the Church, His Bride. This is romance of the highest order. However, many in the church find it so difficult to love either the unsaved or the unlovely, because they cannot love or accept themselves, often because they in turn have not yet been loved.

"We love because He first loved us." (1 John 4:19)

We desperately need this revelation of His love so that we might be healed in our hearts, receive His acceptance and learn to accept ourselves. In turn we can then begin to love and accept others. So much ministry and activity within the Church is motivated by guilt and pressure to perform rather than the motivation of the Father's love operating in and through us. It is time for change!

The Christian life is one of relationship, the Bride with her Bridegroom, this is an issue of the heart. Matthew 15:8-9 declares:

"These people honour me with their lips, but their hearts are far from me. They worship me in vain; their teachings are but rules taught by men."

Our churches are full of people who honour God with their lips, with their time, with their work, with their effort, *but their hearts are far from Him.* Many of us have forsaken intimacy with Jesus because we have dogmatically followed the teachings and believed in the doctrine and traditions of religion that are often nothing more than rules taught by men. If that is the case then there will be no love, no intimacy or relationship with the Saviour Himself, the person Jesus Christ. He remains a remote, distant, ethereal being, one who must be obeyed. We try to live life in the hope that we don't upset Him and instead win sufficient favour to gain entrance into heaven when the inevitable happens. At best we may lay claim, by faith, to His atoning work for our salvation, but we know little of Him and experience nothing of His abiding presence.

Jesus said:

"You diligently study the scriptures because you think by them you will possess eternal life. These are the scriptures that

testify about Me, yet you refuse to come to Me to have life." (John 3:39).

Many of us have forsaken intimacy with the person Jesus and tended to worship our doctrine. Instead of loving God we have revered the Bible, treating the scriptures in an idolatrous way, elevating them above a relationship with Jesus and suffering the inevitable consequence. The Bible is a revelation and a signpost to the person Jesus, it is our relationship with Him that is paramount. The Bible enables us to know Him and understand His ways. It is not God himself.

We have replaced part of the Godhead with things that are indeed valuable to us but are not God. They are often things that have become idols in our lives. We are called to love God the Father, Son and Holy Spirit. However, we may worship God the Father, Son and God our doctrine, or God the Father, Son and God our tradition. Even our ministry, denomination, gifts and calling can replace the very intimacy with the Father for which we were created and redeemed. They can become the driving force of our lives and the object of our passion. The Holy Spirit is calling us back into intimacy with Jesus.

There is a passage of scripture that highlights the condition of much of the Church today. It is found in Song of Solomon 5 and tells of a bride who is awakened by her lover, her bridegroom, knocking on her door. He says to her:

"Open to me, my sister, my darling, my dove, my flawless one. My head is drenched with dew, my hair with the dampness of the night. I have taken off my robe - must I put it on again? I have washed my feet - must I soil them again?"

It appears that the bride doesn't open the door but remains in what I might suggests to be a self-satisfied state, imagining what it would be like for the bridegroom to come in and love her. She doesn't respond, so he knocks again and this time thrusts his hand through the latticework in an attempt to operate the lock from the inside. She tells of how her heart began to pound for him and her hands dripped with myrrh (remember Esther). When she eventually opened the door her lover had gone because she was too slow to respond to him. Her heart sank at his departure and she ran out looking for him but couldn't find him. It was late and because of the way she was dressed the watchman who saw her mistook her for a woman of the night and tragically abused her.

What a terrible story! The bride was longing for her husband and the husband was longing for his bride but she would not respond to him by opening the door. No matter what his desire for her was and what attempts he made to get in, only she had the right to open the door to him. Instead of just imagining what it would be like she could have known him and experienced his love, but instead she ended up being damaged and abused by those who misunderstood her.

In a similar way Jesus spoke very clearly to us in Revelation 3:20, a text often used in evangelism that was actually never written to the unsaved, but to the church of Laodicea, God's own people. This church was described as neither hot nor cold, they thought they were rich but were spiritually barren. They had accumulated material assets but were spiritually bankrupt, naked, blind, deaf and unable to see or hear what God was seeking to communicate. They were neither one thing nor the other, just nominal, they gave allegiance to God with their lips but their hearts were far from Him. God, in His love and mercy, cries out to them:

"Here I am! I stand at the door and knock. If anyone hears my voice and opens the door, I will come in and eat with him and he with Me."

Just like the bride in Song of Solomon the operation of the door of our hearts can only be done from the inside. Jesus is knocking on the door of our hearts, saying, "Here I am, will you let Me in?" Church, if we don't allow Jesus into our hearts, to rule and reign there, we may be rejected because we have lost our first love. We have to let Him be God over our lives, giving Him permission to flood us with His love, grace and mercy, to radically change us and ruin us for anything other than Himself. If we make Him remain outside He may well remove His presence.

The call of God to this generation is to renew that first love of Him, repent of our ungodly control and allow Him, the King of Glory, to come in to love us, heal us, renew us, restore us, and fill us with the power that comes from His Spirit alone. We will then be in a position to offer to the world what we ourselves have received, but until then have very little to give to others.

A Call to Holiness

Holiness is the very nature of God. To be holy is to be like God in His nature. Holiness is to be set apart, consecrated, sanctified, cleansed and purified for God's specific purposes. If we don't like holiness we will not enjoy God, for He is holy. To encounter God is to encounter His holiness. It is impossible to know the Presence of God without knowing His holiness. We cannot just embrace some aspects of the Divine that we are comfortable with whilst circumnavigating the other aspects of His nature. Father is loving, just, righteous, all-powerful and so much more. He is who and what He is; He is holy.

We see the effect of a dramatic encounter with God's holiness when the prophet Isaiah saw the Lord:

"...I saw the Lord, high and exalted, seated on a throne; and the train of his robe filled the temple. Above him were seraphim, each with six wings: With two wings they covered their faces, with two they covered their feet, and with two they were flying. And they were calling to one another:

"Holy, holy, holy is the Lord Almighty; the whole earth is full

of his glory."

At the sound of their voices the doorposts and thresholds shook and the temple was filled with smoke.

"Woe to me!" I cried. "I am ruined! For I am a man of unclean lips, and I live among a people of unclean lips, and my eyes have seen the King, the Lord Almighty." (Isaiah 6:1-5)

When God granted Isaiah a glimpse into heaven his response was immediate. The vision more than took his breath away! He saw things that he found indescribable, - supernatural creatures, the throne of the Almighty. He witnessed an insight into heaven and saw beyond the natural realm into another dimension of creation. He saw the reality of what is outside of, beyond, and yet directly influencing the normative human experience. He was given a vision through a divinely opened portal and saw the Lord, high and exalted, seated on a throne, the train of His robe filling the temple. There is an immediate awareness of the enormity of God. He is so huge, so exalted, far greater than human language can describe. In Isaiah's vision he saw that His royal robe filled the temple. We are taught in the New Testament (1 Corinthians 3:16-17; 6:19) that we, the church, and we as individuals are the temple of the Holy Spirit. If we could see the fullness of the glory and Presence of God filling the Body of Christ, as Isaiah did, what an impact it would make to our confidence, what an impression it would make to our faith and perspective of life, our purpose and our circumstances. Although we may not see it the same manner as Isaiah, it's a truth and a reality nonetheless.

Isaiah continues to relay what he saw. Above the Lord were seraphim, six winged angels of God calling to one another:

"Holy, holy, holy is the Lord God Almighty; the whole earth is filled with His glory."

Their three-fold, tri-directional cry is sometimes considered an acknowledgement of the Triune God, with each "*Holy!*" being directed towards a different member of the Trinity. However, Phil Moore, in his book '*Straight to the Heart of Isaiah*', suggests that above all the repetition serves as a point of emphasis and quality. He points out that when, in 2 Kings 25:15, the writer tries to describe in Hebrew how pure the silver and gold was in the Temple, he uses the expressions "silver, silver" and "gold, gold". The repetition qualifies the gold as the 'goldest' of gold, the most valuable gold, the purest gold imaginable. Likewise, when the seraphim look for a way to describe God's pure holiness, they have to stress an even stronger superlative. God is not just holy and He isn't even holy, holy or really holy. He is in fact holy, holy, holy! Far holier than any language can ever properly describe. It's like describing the Champions League, Europe's premier football competition, comprised of the best of the best teams. Upon reflection you realise that 'champions' falls a little short of reflecting its true quality. So you change its name to the 'Ultimate Champions League', and then realise that even that doesn't seem to do it justice! So you add to it again and again, - the 'Ultimate Champions League of Winners'! The bottom line - it's entirely in a league of its own.

This is what the angels are saying. God is in a league of His own, far greater, higher, holier than the human mind can comprehend. In fact the seraphims covered their eyes with their wings to protect them from the intensity of His brilliant presence.

Isaiah also witnessed that the foundations of heaven shook at the sound of the seraphim's voices and smoke filled the environment.

His immediate response was not some charismatic blessing, rather he began to fall apart at the seams. At the sight of the Almighty he experiences His unfathomable holiness and became deeply convicted of his own unworthiness and sinful nature, realising just how far away he was from God.

'"Woe is me! I am ruined!" he cried.'

He declared that he and his people had unclean lips and wondered how he could still be alive having seen the King, the Lord Almighty. Thank God an angel came and touched his lips with a burning coal from the altar, declaring that his sin had been atoned for and his guilt had been taken away. The angel specifically touched his mouth, the place that Isaiah had become aware was the source of his unholiness. In the light that Jesus said that *"out of the abundance of the heart, so the mouth speaks,"* this would be a fair assumption.

Like Isaiah, when we encounter God as He is, not as we have created or imagined Him to be, we become aware of both His holiness and our own unholiness and need of forgiveness, cleansing and renewal.

Throughout history church revivals have all borne a similar hallmark. As the Holy Spirit intensifies His presence people come under deep conviction and turn to God for salvation. Additionally, God's people are renewed as they too repent from sin and return to the Lord through the cleansing power of the blood of Jesus.

Holiness is one of the non-negotiable requirements in the Kingdom of God. When this is embraced wholeheartedly it is a sure indication that God is drawing close.

In recent years, along with various promises of blessing and power there have been many warnings of judgment falling upon the sin within the Church. By way of illustration, consider the following prophecy written in 1987 by a Pentecostal pastor, David Minor, which has been widely distributed throughout the Church. It is worth referring to at this stage because I think it exemplifies the heart and intent of the Holy Spirit's work within the Church today:

"The Spirit of God would say to you that the wind of the Holy Spirit is blowing through the land. The Church, however, is incapable

of fully recognising this wind. Just as your nation has given names to its hurricanes, so I have put My name on this wind. This wind shall be named 'Holiness unto the Lord'."

"Because of a lack of understanding some of my people will try to find shelter from the wind, but in so doing they shall miss my work. For this wind has been sent to blow through every church that names My name. It shall blow through every institution that has been raised in My name. In those institutions that have substituted their name for Mine, they shall fall by the impact of My wind. Those institutions shall fall like a cardboard shack in a gale. Ministries that have not walked in uprightness before Me shall be broken and fall. For this reason man will be tempted to brand this a work of Satan, but do not be misled. This is My wind."

"I cannot tolerate My Church in its present form, nor will I tolerate it. Ministries and organisations will shake and fall in the face of this wind and even though some will seek to hide from that wind, they shall not escape. It shall blow against your lives and all around you some will appear to be crumbling, and so they shall, but never forget that this is My wind, says the Lord. With tornado force it will come and appear to leave devastation, but the Word of the Lord comes and says "Turn your face into the wind and let it blow. For only that which is not of Me shall be devastated. You must see this as necessary."

"Be not dismayed, for after this my wind shall blow again. Have you not read how My breath blew on the valley of dry bones? So it shall breathe on you. This wind will come in equal force as the first wind. This wind will also have a name. It shall be called 'The Kingdom of God.' It shall bring My power. The supernatural shall come in that wind. The world will laugh at you because of the devastation of the first wind. But they will laugh no more, for this wind will come with force and power that will produce the miraculous among My people and the fear of God shall fall on the nation."

"My people will be willing in the day of My power, says the Lord. In My first wind that is upon you now I will blow out pride, lust, greed, competition and jealousy and you will feel devastated, but haven't you read "blessed are the poor in spirit for theirs is the kingdom of

heaven?" So out of your poverty of spirit I will establish My king-dom."

"Have you not read "the kingdom of God is in the Holy Ghost?" So by My Spirit My kingdom will be established and made manifest."

"Know this also. There will be those who shall seek to hide from this present wind and they will try to flow with the second wind, but they will again be blown away by it. Only those who have turned their faces into the present wind shall be allowed to be propelled by the sec-ond wind."

"You have longed for revival and a return to the miraculous and the supernatural. You and your generation shall see it, but it shall only come by My process, says the Lord. The Church of this nation cannot contain My power in its present form. But as it turns to the wind of the Holiness of God, it shall be purged and changed to contain My glory."

"This is the judgment that has begun with the house of God, but it is not the end. When the second wind has come and brought in My harvest, then shall the end come."

Hebrews 12:25-29 says:

"See to it that you do not refuse him who speaks. If they did not escape when they refused him who warned them on earth, how much less will we, if we turn away from him who warns us from heaven? At that time his voice shook the earth, but now he has prom-ised "Once more I will shake not only the earth but also the heavens." The words 'once more' indicate the removing of what can be shaken - that is, created things - so that what cannot be shaken may remain. Therefore, since we are receiving a kingdom that cannot be shaken, let us be thankful, and so worship God acceptably with reverence and awe, for our "God is a consuming fire.""

We can see that God is intent on bringing the Church into a place of true holiness, which is the very character of God. For a generation or more we have sung songs such as 'Refiner's fire', 'Search my heart oh God' and 'I want to be like Jesus'. Many of us have errantly expected God to simply wave a magic wand over our heads and see holy stardust fall down to make us more like Christ. But the reality is that Holy Spirit will be a refining fire, He will be like wind blowing away chaff and testing the true issues of the heart, for it is out of our heart that our motives, desires, behaviour and lifestyle emanate. He is calling the Church to repentance and exposing our true motives, our level of purity, integrity and general Christlikeness.

Whilst we are so often found to be wanting in these areas, God is offering us a wonderful gift of repentance. Repentance always leads us to freedom, to wholeness and life, but self-justification leads us to death and bondage.

God is turning up the pressure in all of our lives and we are being shaken so that that which does not reflect Christ and His kingdom will fall away and that that which remains will be of value to Him. The sad reality is that many of us cling on to that which God has no real part in, and when His wind blows and shakes these things many will think it is the work of the devil and seek to preserve and protect that which God wants to destroy.

The wind of God not only shakes the things we build and create, - the structures, traditions, methods and religious activities, but He will also shake our lives so that our true mettle can be revealed. God will do whatever it takes to get our attention on the issues that are important to Him, even if we think we have come to the end of our tether and are bewildered by our circumstances. We may try to rebuke the devil or blame others when it is actually the hand of God bringing us to our knees in brokenness and true humility, so that the life of Christ might shine through us and not be obscured by our flesh.

Over the last decade we have seen the exposure of sin within international, high profile Christian ministries. Men and women of God who have enormous gifting have been found with prostitutes or involved in financial misdemeanours. Others continue in pride and arrogance, claiming that the end justifies the means whilst they control and dominate those under their leadership. The Lord is far less interested in what He can do through us compared to what He can do in us. Gifting, no matter how great it is, is always enabled by God for the benefit of others and for His glory. Let's face it, God spoke to one of the prophets through a donkey! He used Jonah, - the most reluctant of prophets, to achieve His own ends. There is very little that we have to glory in ourselves, He is after character, purity, holiness, true love and a motivation in our life and ministry inspired by the Holy Spirit. Our purpose must be to build the kingdom of God and not our own kingdom.

These are without doubt the most challenging of days. God is shaking, refining, blowing, causing the dross in our lives to come to the surface and be wiped off or blown away. This is true revival, God's people coming in repentance, seeking Him for who He is and not for what they can gain from Him, seeking His power and intimacy for a broken world so that we may bring His healing to the nations.

2 Chronicles 7:14 illustrates this so well:

"If My people, who are called by My name, will humble themselves and pray and seek My face and turn from their wicked ways, then will I hear from heaven and will forgive their sin and will heal their land."

The process of revival is quite simple. If God's people, who are called by His name, humble themselves, pray, seek the face of God, turn from **their** wicked ways, then God will hear them from heaven, forgive **their** sins and begin to heal **their** land. The Church has a great responsibility to affect the spiritual climate of a nation. If we want to see God move in our nation, then we must first allow Him to move in our churches. So often our prayers are centred on the sin and brokenness in the world but God first desires to deal with those of us within the Church, those who re-present Him. In order to be a light in a dark world we must first allow God to illuminate the darkness in our own soul and bring transformation in our own lives.

✳ ✳ ✳

God will not be mocked. He is beginning to expose the secret sin of our lives, revealing the true motives of our hearts and calling the Church to holiness through repentance. There is no place to hide when the Holy Spirit begins to move. A farmer sifting his wheat needs a breeze to be blowing so that when he throws the whole grain into the air, the husk blows away leaving the kernel to fall to the ground. The husk is a hard, protective shell around the kernel and I believe that it is the kernel that God wants to reach in our lives. The wind of the Holy Spirit is blowing away the hard husk of self-protection, self-righteousness, self-vindication and self-justification. To be honest, most of us need this to be a sovereign work of God because we are so often beguiled regarding what is or isn't of God. We, like David in Psalm 51, must cry out:

"Create in me a pure heart, O God."

It can only be a sovereign work of God to renew our hearts to be like His. We must therefore open ourselves up to the power of the wind of God blowing through our lives in order to cause the husks around us to be blown away. The pruned fruit of our lives will then fall into the hand of the Father so that we can be resown, available to fulfil His plans and purposes under His anointing and according to His will and purpose.

Healing

"The Spirit of the Sovereign Lord is on me, because the Lord

has anointed me to preach good news to the poor. He has sent me to bind up the broken-hearted, to proclaim freedom for the captives and release from darkness for the prisoners, to proclaim the year of the Lord's favour and the day of vengeance of our God, to comfort all who mourn, and provide for those who grieve in Zion – to bestow on them a crown of beauty instead of ashes, the oil of gladness instead of mourning, and a garment of praise instead of a spirit of despair. They will be called oaks of righteousness, a planting of the Lord for the display of His splendour." (Isaiah 61:1-3)

Just as the earlier prophesy spoke of a first wind of the Holy Spirit called 'holiness' and a second wind called 'the kingdom of God', I believe the refining work of the Holy Spirit will initially put His finger on issues of holiness in the Church, followed by an expression of the power of the kingdom of God hitherto unknown in human history. This will include along with it healing and wholeness. The passage above reflects the very heart and intent of God to bless creation with abundance, to work miracles of healing and deliverance, and to confront religiosity and release true spiritual life.

It isn't until we love the broken and wounded in the same way that Jesus does, with the compassion of His heart, that we will begin to see the power of God moving.

Unfortunately, the reality is that we are often like the disciples who, although they had seen Jesus transfigured in glory on the mountain, still could not cast a demon out of a young boy due to their unbelief. The Church, by and large, is impotent in the area of healing, deliverance and effective evangelism. I believe that following this refining wind of the Spirit there will come a move of God's power that to date we have been unable to handle due to our pride and self-centredness. It isn't until we love the broken and wounded in the same way that Jesus does, with the compassion of His heart, that we will begin to see the power of God moving.

We have to veer away from building our own ministry and move towards exercising the ministry of Jesus into the lives of others. We may have an intellectual comprehension of this, but God sees into our hearts. I believe there is a burning desire in the heart of the Father to touch the physically broken, damaged, wounded and the emotionally and mentally sick with a power to heal and deliver that can only come from Him. This ministry is not an optional extra for the Church, but very much part of Her responsibility in bringing healing and full salvation to those within Her ranks.

It has been said that the Church is an army, a hospital and a family. I believe this is true, and each of us should find church a safe place to grow, learn and develop. We are called to be an army that will touch the world for Jesus Christ and demonstrate the power of the Kingdom of Heaven. We are also called to be a hospital, a place of refuge and healing. Some seem to like staying in hospital, constantly going from one sickness to another, but hospitals are a place to visit not dwell, and health should be valued above repeated healing. We are called to be a family; a place of mutual love, safety, fellowship and belonging.

I was once speaking at a church on the south coast of England and during the ministry time a lady within the fellowship came forward to receive from the Lord. As I was praying for her it became apparent that she could not hear, so I prayed that God would heal her ears in the name of Jesus. A couple of months after this event I received a letter from her saying she had been surprised I'd prayed for her hearing as she had never thought of asking God to heal her. She thought it was something she just had to carry throughout her life. To her amazement, very early the following morning, the sound of the birds singing outside her bedroom window woke her up! God had gloriously and wonderfully healed her completely from her deafness.

Another lady came to us for help who had a background in witchcraft and had suffered severe mental and emotional damage as a consequence. This dear lady had been receiving help from various people including a psychiatrist and Christian counsellors. Although improvements had been made, she was still living in torment, fear and guilt. She had no real intimate relationship with God, although she knew He was her only hope. With the cooperation of the church, two of our team ministered to her, expelling the demonic and bringing healing to her damaged emotions. We assured her of Gods forgiveness and acceptance and built her up in faith with the truth of God's Word. Within 36 hours this woman had been set free to such a measure that she could hardly contain her joy and liberty. As she began to tell others what God had done in her life, a broad smile on her face and a sparkle in her eyes demonstrated the power and reality of God in setting captives free. It is the responsibility of the Church to bring healing to those who are saved, in every area of their being, and the Lord will work with those who are willing to work with Him in this regard.

When I first came to Christ back in 1975 I was suffering from crippling anxiety, panic attacks and depression. At that time I couldn't find a Church or minister who could help me, - some considered my suffering as my cross to bear and others told me that Jesus didn't heal today. However I believed Jesus was the same yesterday, today and forever. I read in the scriptures that Jesus went around doing good and healing all who were oppressed of the devil (Acts 10:38) and I was convinced that Jesus had not changed, that He was still a freedom fighter bringing healing and deliverance to those who were suffering. Against all the odds, in so far as there were no Christians that I knew who believed the bible as I believed it, I went forward for ministry at a gathering of young Christians. The man leading the meeting said, "I believe God wants to give peace to someone here today." I knew that he was referring to me but I was very scared about being vulnerable and going forward. I was in a terrible state of panic as fear gripped me and I wanted to run out of the room because I felt so claustrophobic. However, I summoned up courage and the man prayed a very simple prayer over me; - "Dear Jesus, I ask you to give Clive peace that passes all understanding and fill him with your Holy Spirit." I felt something leave me on my breath, a sigh and then a sense of calm and peace came upon me. In an instant the power of fear that had crippled me for so many years was broken. I believe that spirits of fear had entered me through my generational line and then been compounded by my years of rebellion and wandering, by associating with the wrong people and getting involved in all kinds of immorality, violence, drink and drugs. These became open doors for the enemy to enter and control many aspects of my life. When I accepted Christ as my Saviour and Lord I was then in a position to receive the effective ministry that is available to all followers of Jesus. This amazing deliverance was without fuss or drama yet incredibly powerful. The power and control of the enemy was broken, enabling me to walk out of bondage through both the renewing of my mind and emotional healing.

As a result of my own experience I felt drawn towards bringing full salvation to others. I not only preached the gospel but demonstrated its reality by ministering in the power of the Holy Spirit to the whole person; spirit, soul and body. I have subsequently been involved in various healing ministries and led our own ministry in equipping the saints to move naturally in the supernatural of God. Over the years we have also had the privilege of running many training courses across many denominations in the Body of Christ.

When I was first saved healing was not embraced in as many churches as it is today. Perhaps some Pentecostal churches prayed for the sick as a matter of course, but by and large most main-line denominations either did not have the vision for healing and wholeness on their radar, or were not sure how to go about doing it or where to obtain help. Over time various specialised healing centres began to emerge and nowadays far more churches have their own ministry teams available to pray for healing. There is also a vast array of material now available to help equip God's people in this regard. Regrettably, a radical vision and expectation for Jesus to supernaturally heal and deliver still seems to be generally lacking within the Church but I do believe that the tide is turning and there is an increase in desire to know the power of God and wield the tools to bring healing and wholeness.

I am convinced that it is God's will and purpose to bring holiness to the Church, to inspire our hearts and give faith for healing and wholeness as a demonstration of the Father's love that, in turn, confirms the message of the Kingdom of God.

There are, of course, reasons why Jesus heals today and calls us to share in this ministry. We know that He taught in the synagogues, preached the good news of the Kingdom of Heaven, called people to repentance and faith toward God, healed every disease and sickness and that the crowds followed Him. Isaiah the prophet saw that healing would be a hallmark of Messiah and Jesus certainly fulfilled that criteria (Lk. 4:18). John the Baptist also recognised healing to be an authentication of Messiah's credentials. The question therefore arises, - 'Why did Jesus heal?' After all, Jesus could have lived a pure and holy life, free from sin, preaching and teaching and laying down His life by dying on the cross to work atonement for our sins. Wasn't this more than enough? Why was healing such a prominent aspect of His life and ministry? I suggest four reasons.

Firstly, healing and deliverance demonstrate who He is. His sonship of the Father, His divinity and His authority as King of kings. Jesus said:

"If I drive out demons by the finger of God, the kingdom of God has come upon you." (Luke 11:20)

Jesus confirmed the truth of His words by demonstrating a supernatural power that accompanied His teaching:

"Believe me when I say I am in the Father and the Father is in me; or at least believe on the evidence of the miracles themselves." (John 14:11-12)

Healing, signs and wonders were the hallmark of His ministry. The apostle Paul said:

"When I came to you brothers, I did not come with eloquence or superior wisdom as I proclaimed to you the testimony of God. For I resolved to know nothing while I was with you except Jesus Christ and Him crucified. I came to you in weakness and fear, and with trembling. My message and my preaching were not with persuasive words, but with a demonstration of the Spirit's power, so your faith might not rest on men's wisdom, but on God's power." (1 Cor 2:1-5)

Paul obviously realised that a demonstration of divine power was needed to reinforce the message that he carried and today too we need a demonstration of divine power to reinforce and authenticate the message that we carry. It may be the only thing that convinces people of the reality of God and His pursuit of them. May God give us greater boldness to believe Him for the impossible and to minister faithfully healing in Jesus' name as part of our ministry.

Many think of Jesus as a mild mannered fellow and to be honest rather dull and benign. However this is not how scripture reveals Him at all. In fact 1 John 3:8 says:

"...The reason the Son of God appeared was to destroy the devil's work."

Jesus came to undo, destroy, and reverse the enemy's work in human life. All the sin, the damage, the pain and suffering. Everything that has resulted in the fall of man where the enemy has been given free rein to enter and wreak havoc in all of creation, including the human experience. The deception, the darkness of human reasoning, the cruelty and quest for power, fame, possessions and unbridled pleasure. All that sin has corrupted, fuelled and influenced by satanic forces, Jesus has come to destroy. Scripture tells us that the demonic powers behind the chaos and turmoil, have been disarmed by Christ on the cross and that He has triumphed over them (Colossians 10:4). Jesus expressed the Father's power and demonstrated the rule of heaven here on earth and we are called to the fight, to continue what Christ has secured and started, - to uproot, tear down and overthrow so that we can then build and plant. We have been given all of the resources needed to advance the Kingdom of God through the power of the Holy Spirit. We have been given the right and the authority of a true son of God:

"Yet to all who did receive Him, to those who believed in His name, He gave the right to become children of God." (John 1:12)

We have been given the same power of the Holy Spirit that raised Christ from the dead:

"I have given you authority to trample on snakes and scorpions and to overcome all the power of the enemy; nothing will harm you." (Luke 10:19).

God has equipped us with the tools to do the job in His name:

"The weapons we fight with are not the weapons of the world. On the contrary, they have divine power to demolish strongholds." (2 Cor 10:4-5)

We are well equipped with the resources of heaven within us and at our disposal to continue the fight, set captives free and usher in the healing power of heaven here on earth.

It would appear too that Holy Spirit is committed to restoring people back to wholeness, bringing us back to an original condition. This is a powerful motivation for God to heal. Isaiah prophesied that Messiah would give us beauty for ashes, the oil of joy for mourning and a garment of praise for a spirit of despair (Isa. 61:3). The Father is committed to restoring our lives from all of the brokenness of inherited sin and the damage caused by life's experience.

"He restores my soul." (Psalm 23:3)

To restore is to rebuild us back to our original design and condition. This process is often a journey of divine therapy, allowing Holy Spirit to unpick the past, heal the pain, cleanse and free us from pollutants in the soul, refresh us with His Spirit and enable us to rediscover our true identity, secure and whole in Christ. He loves to do this and invites us to respond to His leading into true freedom on the inside.

When Jesus encountered a leper in Mark 1:40-42 the leper asked if Jesus was willing to make him clean. Jesus' response was:

'...[Jesus was] moved with compassion, He reached out his hand and touched the man. "I am willing," He said. "Be clean!" Immediately the leprosy left him and he was cleansed.'

Compassion seems to be the heart motivation behind the healing ministry of the divine. Father's love is demonstrated in power. His motive is love and compassion. He has the ability and willingness to accomplish what He loves to do - to heal, restore, mend, and set free. All of this reveals and demonstrates what God is like, and we are called, as the body of Christ, to be His hands, His voice, His arms of love that heal a broken world.

Equipping

There is a change in the landscape of the church in this

generation. What we have traditionally understood to be the way of doing things within our churches is shifting.

Church transpires and develops in the wake of mission. It is shaped according to the nature of the people and expressed through their unique gifts, temperament and aspirations.

I believe there is now a greater emphasis for sending out into the harvest rather than drawing believers together into ever enlarging congregations. This reflects the heart of God who gave away His Son (John 3:16), commanded us to go (Matthew 28), and as yet has not said stop! The church is meant to be the consequence of mission rather than just entertaining mission as part of its program. Church transpires and develops in the wake of mission. It is shaped according to the nature of the people and expressed through their unique gifts, temperament and aspirations.

❋ ❋ ❋

The balance of missional thrust and building the Body of Christ is held in a tension, therefore we must take note and understand how God has designed us to realise both objectives.

"It was he who gave some to be apostles, some to be prophets, some to be evangelists and some to be pastors and teachers, to prepare Gods people for works of service, so that the Body of Christ may be built up." (Eph 4:11)

These people, raised up by God, are ministry gifts to the church, namely; - apostles, prophets, pastors teachers and evangelists. Their primary role is to equip God's people to enable the building up of the Body of Christ. There has been some misunderstanding concerning what these ministry gifts actually are and what is their role and function.

Firstly it is important to grasp that their purpose is to equip God's people and not to be doing things on behalf of the church. If the latter mindset dominates then these people become a bottle neck instead of a gateway. The idea is that these gifts equip the church to do works that are apostolic, prophetic, evangelistic, pastoral and educational through teaching, modelling and releasing, preferably by anointing, commissioning and supporting.

Secondly it is important to understand what each of these ministry gifts actually do.

The apostle is one who is sent to pioneer into uncharted territory. They cross borders and boundaries, finding a way through resistance to establish the kingdom of God by laying foundations upon which others can build. It is like hacking a way through the jungle to create a basic path which future travellers can develop into a road. There is often a fathering nature to this call as their primary role will be to form Christ in those who follow them, that they in turn will become true sons of the Father, ready to father their own sons in the faith. This fathering is not only for upcoming apostles but for the whole Body of Christ, that they would be seen as the founding fathers of their faith in Christ.

An apostle is not an overseer of a group of churches, that is the role of a bishop, which by its nature provides pastoral leadership. An apostle is a pioneer who develops that same pioneering nature in those he leads, and teaches, trains and equips those called to such ministry.

Signs and wonders are the hallmark of the apostles ministry because their call requires the supernatural to accomplish their task, which will always be way beyond their natural gift-ing and ability. Miracles are required to enable the advance-ment of the Kingdom of God.

When the Iron Curtain first started coming down I was one of many who took the initiative and went into Eastern Europe to preach the gospel. On one occasion I was with a team in Talin, Estonia, ministering among the Russian people there. We had been asked to collect books and bibles that had been translated into Russian from a nearby printer, ready for distri-bution into the churches by our local contact. Unfortunately the day we arrived at the printing company it was closed due to the currency changing from the Russian Ruble into the Estonian Kroon. Everything was shut down to enable people to organise themselves with the new currency. Along with another team member we knocked on the door of the printers and after a while a lady opened it and very angrily shouted to us in Es-tonian that they were closed. Through the translator I asked if it would be possible to collect our books and bibles but she imme-diately replied "no!" I asked again and she said "no" even louder and began to close the door on us. I then said in English, which I am sure she didn't understand, "I command you to give us the bible and books that we have come for. I bind the powers of darkness resisting us and tell you to release that which belongs to us, in Jesus name." I said it all with a smile and using tones that were soft but expressed the authority that comes from heaven in Jesus Christ. She continued to shout "no", telling us it could not be done, whilst simultaneously walking in and out of the office, collecting the goods and passing them across the doorway to us! As we loaded the many boxes on to the await-ing bus our team inside the vehicle rejoiced at the breakthrough that God had given us.

On the same mission trip we held meetings in a hall used for funerals; the only place that the locals could find available. During one of our meetings a witch found her way in and began to disturb the meeting by screaming insults and cursing us in English. We discovered that his woman knew no English whatsoever but the demonic was communicating to us, through her, in our own language. I asked the worship team to begin leading us in song and during this time two of my team, one lady doctor along with my father in law, Mel, went to see the lady and began to bind the demonic in her. There was no translator near them so they spoke in English to the demons as worship ascended to Jesus! The woman manifested and was set free by God's power. With the help of the (now present) translator she then gave her heart and life to the Lord, thanking God for setting her free and saving her.

At that same event a young man who had broken his leg the previous day was instantly healed. He arrived at our meeting on the following day without a cast and able to move freely and without pain.

"Today Holy Spirit is seeking those who are willing to be trained and form part of an end-time army, a body impassioned, motivated and equipped to do the works to which God has called us."

During this pioneering mission many found faith in Christ and many were healed. We were able to give locally translated bibles and christian literature to the people, and we had the privilege of encouraging and supporting leaders of the local churches who themselves were only recent converts to Christ.

Today Holy Spirit is seeking those who are willing to be trained and form part of an end-time army, a body impassioned, motivated and equipped to do the works to which God has called us.

The day of ministry teams doing things on behalf of the

local church is over, it is a day for giving ourselves to ministerial development and presenting ourselves as living sacrifices. (Romans 12:1-2)

In the first year that I was saved I attended a large Christian meeting at Westminster Central Hall in London, to hear a speaker named George Verwer, the leader of Operation Mobilisation. The impact of that meeting remains with me today, - more than 40 years on. He preached on Romans 12:1-2:

"Therefore I urge you, brothers, in view of Gods mercy, to offer your bodies as living sacrifices, holy and pleasing to God - this is your spiritual act of worship. Do not be conformed any longer to the pattern of this world, but be transformed by the renewing of your mind."

As he preached on this passage, I felt Holy Spirit stir deeply within me and I was challenged at the way I had become moulded into the ways of the world. I held the same ambitions and aspirations, all with no eternal value, mostly selfish in motive and futile in the eternal perspective of things. He then spoke about world missions, God's heart for the nations and asked who would be willing to break the mould of the world and lay their own life down for a bigger cause than a career or worldly pleasure. He shared how Christ had laid His life down for me and for the world and was looking for those who would take up the challenge and allow their life to be an act of worship, acceptable to God, by giving themselves to the cause of Christ and the advancement of His kingdom. I jumped out of my seat and nearly flattened a few people as I rushed to the front of the auditorium, utterly ruined for anything other than Christ and His cause. I wanted my life to amount to something, to have meaning and purpose. I realised that God had called me and given me a destiny to be a freedom fighter and to set people free from their sin, from satan and even from themselves through the power of the cross. That day I gave my life to Jesus without conditions, I laid it down at the cross for Him to use me as He saw fit, for His glory and the extension of His kingdom. Not receiving Him just as my saviour but also making Him my Lord, I gave Him back the life He had won for me. I was never the same again and can honestly say that there has never been a day since when I have regretted making that decision or relinquishing control to the Father, trusting Him to realise His dream for me and through me.

Maybe it is a time to consider our walk with God. Is the relationship you have with God based solely on what you can get out of it? Try considering what you can give to God rather than focusing on what you receive. God is calling you to re-examine your life in the light of Romans 12:1-2. Re-present yourself afresh to Him as a living sacrifice, give your life to Christ, let go of your control and submit to His Lordship. Stop conforming to this world's value system and begin to embrace the true values of the kingdom of heaven here on earth.

✻ ✻ ✻

The traditional model of church within many denominations has been for pastor to be all things to all people, - an impossible task which sets them up for failure. Pastors are too often required to operate like the CEO of a corporation rather than being a source of life and power flowing from the Father and resourcing the church.

The congregation has to move from simply being spectators to become involved in active service within the army of God. The Church requires crew, not more passengers!

"We would all agree to this principle but how many of us are actively prioritising

the enabling of God's people by showing them how to 'do the stuff?'"

However, where to get equipped can be a challenge. Our bible colleges are great at educating us in theology, but often spend little time teaching the more practical ministry essentials. How do we move naturally in the supernatural of God? How do we hear the voice of God for ourselves and others? How should we do basic prayer ministry, or counselling? How and when should we minister healing and deliverance?

Everyone has a vital part to play, not just in the church structure, but within the sphere that God has placed us, - in schools, universities, factories, offices, hospitals, neighbourhoods etc. We are called to be salt, light, yeast, a natural witness and a source of divine light influencing those we spend our time with, equipped to minister effectively when required by Holy Spirit. We would all agree to this principle but how many of us are actively prioritising the enabling God's people by showing them how to 'do the stuff?' Perhaps our time together in church might prove more fruitful if we adjusted our program to line-up with the intent of the Father and trained an army useful in the hand of God. This has to be preferable to maintaining, what at times, looks likes a pen full of overfed sheep who seem to be constantly bleating, demanding more and more attention or church style entertainment but never seeming to personally change.

God is on the move. Much of our church activity will become increasingly redundant as Holy Spirit reorganises His church to realise His vision of a dark world invaded by those bearing His presence and ministering in His love and power. Freedom fighters, radical truth proclaimers, compassionate healers, all on fire with the Holy Spirit, changing atmospheres and bringing salvation to those in darkness and recovery to those damaged by the adverse effects of life in a broken world.

Preparation - A Priority for positioning and purpose

"It comes down to the powerful, sudden realisation that you have come to this royal position for a time such as this. This is your defining moment, will you be equal to the task?"

The story of Esther unfolds. Following her long preparation she is presented to and accepted by the King:

"Now the king was more attracted to Esther than any of the other women, and she won the favour and approval more than any of the other virgins. So he set a royal crown on her head and made her queen instead of Vashti." (Esther 2:17)

Esther now found herself in a position of privilege, power and intimacy with the King, a long way from her beginnings as an orphan in a strange and alien land. During this time, Hamen, one of the kings closest members of his court plotted to destroy the Jews living in the land because Mordecai refused to bow down to him. Hamen was consumed with self-interest and pride and flattered at the position the King had given him but was obviously grieved with Mordecai, against whom he held a grudge. Hamen conspired to get the king to sign an edict ordering the destruction of the Jews, but when Mordecai heard of this he humbled himself before God, he began deep intercession, tearing his clothes, putting on sackcloth and ashes and entered the city wailing loudly. He sent word to queen Esther, asking her to go to the King to plead for mercy on behalf of their people, the Jews. Esther reported back to Mordecai that she had not been invited to enter the Kings presence for over a month and that to do so uninvited would mean certain death. The only time anyone would survive such behaviour was if the King pointed the sceptre he held towards the uninvited guest. This showed his acceptance and favour, enabling them to approach. Mordecai sent this answer back to Esther:

"Do not think that because you are in the king's house you alone of all the Jews will escape. For if you remain silent at this time, relief and deliverance for the Jews will arise from another place, but you and your father's family will perish. And who knows but that you have come to royal position for such a time as this?"

This challenge from Mordecai puts everything into perspective. In other words, he is reminding Esther that her being chosen from obscurity, poverty and wretchedness was far more than merely setting her apart to be prepared for the king. This was not all about her pleasure and beautification alone. It was not just to train her in royal ways to understand the protocol of the royal court. Her preparation was for a purpose, her elevation was to uniquely position her for a specific task that God required of her. It comes down to the powerful, sudden realisation that you have come to this royal position for a time such as this. This is your defining moment, will you be equal to the task?

Her response is quite beautiful. I imagine this tender young woman, vulnerable, afraid of the enormity of the task, now placed into a position to intercede before the king on behalf of her people. With the risk of losing everything she has attained and possibly even her life, she bravely responds:

"I will go to the king, even though it is against the law. And if I perish, I perish."

Esther became willing to lay her life down for her God and His people. This echoes the sentiments of Revelations 12:11, which tells us:

"They overcame him (that is the devil) *by the blood of the lamb and by the word of their testimony; they did not love their lives so much as to shrink back from death."*

The true, powerful, effective, overcoming ministry of the Church is done through those who lay their lives down at the cross and die to their own ambition and pride, who refuse to shrink back from adversity and stand in the face of the enemy, willing even to die rather than flinch or run away, so that we may apply the blood through the word of our testimony and overcome the darkness with the light of Christ.

Our positioning is vital to the cause of Christ and the extension of His kingdom. We must realise that the favour, blessing and honour on our lives is not only a hallmark and reality of being a true son of God, but it is also a means to an end, not an end in itself.

To bring this home, the question arises, where are we as individuals? What mountain are you willing to die on? In other words, what are you willing to give your life for? I guess most of us would be willing to give our lives for our family or even close friends, but beyond the obvious, relational bonds to which we are committed, what cause are we willing to give ourselves to? What location? What group of people? What movement? What on earth are we willing to die for because it means that much to us, it holds such value to us that we are willing to give all that we are and all we have?

"Greater love has no one than this, than to lay down one's life for his friends." (John 15:13)

I am persuaded that much of the insipid nature of Christian religion and the ineffectiveness of local church in their respective communities may simply be because we don't love people enough or care for them to the same extent that God cares. This love and commitment comes through divine revelation. If we have not received a revelation or been impacted by God's massive grace and desire for where we have been planted, 'for a time such as this,' then we will be looking for the exit when things get tough or no longer suit us.

A few years ago, and this story is not an isolated incident, a young man joined a church Karen and I planted in Lancaster, UK. He was very impressive and quickly won our hearts. He initiated many good works and was being identified as future leadership material. After I had preached on this subject one Sunday morning he came to me, somewhat emotional, and said "This church is the mountain that I am willing to die on." He indicated that he wanted to serve in this church and offered his whole-self to work with us, that whatever the cost this was where God had called him to plant roots and to grow. Not too long after this a better job offer came along and he relocated, never to be seen or heard of again! I have even had those with whom I have shared leadership offering this same depth of commitment and loyalty, only to suddenly abandon the church and their responsibilities to those they served without any prior warning. My point is that most of us make emotional decisions rather than considering what God is truly asking of us. His requirement may be that we endure, be disciplined, or accept that circumstances are not ideal for a season rather than concerning ourselves with what may or may not make us happy.

"You will never truly know who is willing to give their life for the cause until they are actually required to do so."

In contrast to the aforementioned, I have experienced a depth of loyalty and covering from some of those who minister with me even when they are feeling dissatisfied. There have been times when I have felt so weak and vulnerable, even on my knees wanting to give up, and they have gathered around and shielded me with prayer and companionship. Even though they did not have solutions they stood loyal until we worked things through. It would have been so far from their minds to consider abdicating the responsibilities they been entrusted with. True shepherds give their lives for the sheep, but hired hands are sometimes in it for what they can get out of it, their motives shrouded in religious jargon. You will never truly know who is willing to give their life for the cause until they are actually required to do so.

"It takes audacious faith and a willingness to lose everything to advance from where we are to where God wants to take us. Often the key is whether we are willing to pay the price, to take the risk, and to endure until the breakthrough comes."

Esther proved faithful. She took courage and entered, unannounced, into the presence of the King. As she approached the King turned to look at her, he pointed his sceptre toward her, permissioning her to come towards him. Again she found favour through her boldness and faith, and only now, in this place of intimacy, was she able to intercede on behalf of her people. God gave her divine wisdom and a strategy to overcome Hamen and his corrupt plan. Hamen came to an abrupt and humiliating end, God's people were saved, and Mordecai and Esther were elevated and honoured more than they could ever have expected.

It takes audacious faith and a willingness to lose everything to advance from where we are to where God wants to take us. Often the key is whether we are willing to pay the price, to take the risk, and to endure until the breakthrough comes.

BLESSED ARE THOSE INVITED TO THE CELEBRATION

Celebration is an important part of being human. It is natural to celebrate achievements, victories, the passing of seasons and welcoming of new ones. I recall seeing newsreels of exuberant crowds dancing, shouting, hugging, drinking and laughing in Piccadilly Circus and Trafalgar Square in London following the announcement that the Second World War was over. Most didn't know how best to express their joy so they went wild along with everyone else in the streets. We celebrate birthdays, anniversaries, graduations, Christmas, Easter, harvest and so much more.

A few years ago Karen and I celebrated 25 years of marriage. We invited our family and close friends to join us in marking the occasion and we had a wonderful time. We not only marked our wedding anniversary but celebrated life together! Many went out of their way to be with us, some travelling huge distances, and their commitment spoke volumes about the importance of family and friendship. They were willing to inconvenience themselves to invest in our bonds of relationship. We also had a huge amount of fun, great food, music, dancing, games and lots of hugs and laughter. Celebration is important to us all, it binds us together, helps us feel good and creates precious memories.

In my lifetime I have been aware of many significant moves of God around the world. Whether we call them revivals, renewals, or something else, they have proved to be of great impact to the Church.

One move that I was particularly close to was the Father's Blessing which flowed from Toronto in 1994. Mainly due to my relationship with its leaders prior to that time I enjoyed the fellowship and experience of God through this phenomenal outpouring of the Holy Spirit. This move of God impacted so many people and at times caused many to be overcome with hysterical laughter, exhibiting apparently drunken behaviour, light-heartedness, deep peace, assurance, security and a general blessing of the Father. This, of course, is nothing new. Throughout history these manifestations appeared during intense moves of God among His people. Even on the Day of Pentecost when the disciples of Jesus were impacted by the Holy Spirit, they were thought to be drunk! The apostle Peter had to explain that what they were witnessing was in fact the fulfilment of prophecy:

"This is what was spoken by the prophet Joel". (Acts 2:15-17)

Peter anchored the experience in scripture to validate that what was happening was under divine inspiration and totally in line with God's will and purpose. It was, of course, a huge shock to the people who were not used to outbursts of demonstrative behaviour, particularly within a religious context.

However, now, just as then, to some this proves to be an offence, to others it may be considered demonic. It seemed inappropriate to them that such behaviour was displayed in a church setting, but the religious mind is often offended by the Holy Spirit. Certainly, Jesus was a constant challenge to the religious leaders of His day. They could not accept that He was from God because He didn't operate according to their traditions or come under their control. I am confident that not all that has gone on in any significant move of the Holy Spirit has pleased the Father, mainly due to our human responses, choices and behaviour. Our tendency is invariably to welcome the divine initiative and enter in to embrace the new experience. In our enthusiasm and eagerness for it to perpetuate and increase we develop learned behaviour that soon becomes our new religious culture. What certainly started in the Spirit may slip into a work of the flesh in our desperation for it not to end. This, in turn, can open us up to all kinds of demonic deceptions, for we know that our adversary may come disguised as an angel of light. The counterfeit experience may create similar emotional responses and seem plausible, but in fact is a forgery of the original, genuine ministry of the Holy Spirit.

To my delight, those I know who have led much of this particular move of God have not only had such a hunger for the Holy Spirit but also lengthy experience in ministry. They soon sense the false and the flesh, and when mistakes were made they had the humility to redress the situation and get back in line with the true leading of the Holy Spirit. Humility, honesty, sensitivity and courage are key in all of this.

I believe that any significant move of God needs to be celebrated. In fact, much of what we have experienced in recent years is a prophetic foretaste of what is yet to come. This outpouring of the Father's blessing is pointing us towards the return of Jesus to take His Bride into the marriage supper of the Lamb. It will be the biggest party the world has ever seen and the greatest celebration of all time.

God has written into scripture types and shadows of what has been and what is yet to be fulfilled in Christ. We consider many of the Old Testament characters to be types of Christ. Not least of all Adam (Rom. 5:14), King David, Moses, Joseph etc. Also events like the preservation of Noah during the flood, the redemption of Israel from Egypt (1 Corinthians 10:11), the tabernacle, sacrifice, sabbath etc. are all shadows, copies, of the heavenly reality, fulfilled in Christ (Hebrews 9:11-12; 10:19-20).

It is therefore quite reasonable for us to look at the book

of Esther and see much by way of types and shadows of Christ. In particular, the work of the Holy Spirit illustrated in Esther helps us to recognise what He is doing in and through the Church in preparation for the return of the Bridegroom. Much of this we have already discussed.

In the light of this, consider Xerxes' great celebration and the refusal of his queen, Vashti, to attend. To add insult to injury, Vashti chose to throw her own party, separate and independent from her King. Doesn't this speak to us contemporarily of those who refuse to respond to the invitation of King Jesus? By contrast, we see Esther, a nobody, an orphan, a foreigner in an alien land, poor and yet chosen from among the rest to enter the King's palace. Esther responded to the king's invitation and became queen. She was uniquely and strategically positioned for the benefit of God's people...

"...for a time such as this".

These two characters perfectly illustrate two kinds of people in the Kingdom of God. Those who enjoy the position of privilege, position and power, yet use all that is provided for them to indulge in a self-centred life, responding to the King only when it suits them. Ultimately, they are rejected and do not enter into the fullness of their unrealised potential or the joy of the Lord. Jesus warns in Matthew 7:21-23:

"Not everyone who says to me, 'Lord, Lord,' will enter the kingdom of heaven, but only the one who does the will of my Father who is in heaven. Many will say to me on that day, 'Lord, Lord, did we not prophesy in your name and in your name drive out demons and in your name perform many miracles?' Then I will tell them plainly, 'I never knew you. Away from me, you evildoers!'"

Scripture gives clear warning that even those who operate under divine power may not be in right relationship with Him or share in the eternal inheritance.

In contrast are the 'Esthers', those who have no ambition for self-aggrandisement but keep saying "yes" to God. Esther responded in obedience to every command given to her, submitted to those overseeing her and embraced every opportunity afforded to her. Through this process she became queen and proved beneficial and fruitful for the kingdom of God. This is not an unfamiliar theme in scripture. There are many occasions where those who found themselves in dire circumstances experienced God's favour because of their ongoing obedience to Him. Joseph, David, Abraham and Gideon, amongst others, and prime examples of this heart-attitude.

❊ ❊ ❊

We looked previously at the story Jesus told of the King who sent out invites to attend the wedding celebration of his son. Each guest in turn refused his invitation and, like Vashti, rather than pleasing the King, set about doing what was more important to them, prioritising what would ultimately benefit them most. The King, enraged, rejected them and instructed his servants to go out into the areas of darkness and invite those, like Esther, who would never have expected an invitation to a royal banquet. The hungry and thirsty gladly accepted the opportunity for good food and drink, and, although not fit for a palace, they responded and entered into all that the king had for them.

We have also recalled the story of the lost son. When he returned home his father threw a huge celebration, accepting him entirely on the basis of grace and unconditional acceptance. Remember how the elder son refused to enter in to the celebrations? Even though the father pleaded for him to join them his hard heart was set to stay outside and reject the father's invitation. He was either unable, but more than likely unwilling, to embrace grace, generosity of heart and acceptance.

When the apostle John shared the words of Christ to the Church in the book of Revelation he said:

"... he that has ears to hear let him hear what the Spirit is saying to the church."

This not only tells us that Christ is communicating, but also that there is the potential for us not to hear if our ears are not listening for His voice. Sometimes we don't have ears to hear because we prefer the sound of our own voice. We say yes to our own desires, ambitions and preferences and say no to God if we feel that His word doesn't line up with our priorities.

In these last days we must be willing to obey the command of the King and choose to recognise that Christ knows the end from the beginning. He knows what is best for us in every situation, even when circumstances look hopeless and what He is asking seems unreasonable or illogical at the time. The consequence of obedience is true anointing and fruitfulness.

✻ ✻ ✻

The book of Ecclesiastes 3:1-8 tells us that there is a time for all things:

"There is a time for everything, and a season for every activity under the heavens: a time to be born and a time to die, a time to plant and a time to uproot, a time to kill and a time to heal, a time to tear down and a time to build, a time to weep and a time to laugh, a time to mourn and a time to dance, a time to scatter stones and a time to gather them, a time to embrace and a time to refrain from embracing, a time to search and a time to give up, a time to keep and a time to

throw away, a time to tear and a time to mend, a time to be silent and a time to speak, a time to love and a time to hate, a time for war and a time for peace."

Knowing the times and seasons is key to preventing us from reaping when we should be sowing or mourning when it is time to dance. Being in step with God's agenda is vital. Sensitivity to the Holy Spirit is essential. Knowing His voice is paramount.

One of our greatest challenges in life is understanding the times and seasons of God in relation to our particular circumstances. We have a tendency of imposing our own agenda, rooted in our own perspective, onto our own or other peoples' situations. However, if we are in tune with God's agenda, if we are seeing things from His heavenly perspective and responding in obedience to that truth, irrespective of whatever season we may find ourselves in we will be doing what is right and appropriate in God's eyes because we are operating in alignment with Him.

If God offers us a season to enter into a foretaste of His joy, extravagant love and grace, a time to enjoy Him and one another in a celebration of life and divine generosity, we would do well to embrace it. However, if we enter into a season of stress, challenge and difficulty, it is not that God is abandoning us. He may be positioning us for greater victory and fruitfulness. This is when we must tap deep into our spiritual resources to journey through troubled waters. Seasons change and we need to adapt accordingly, just as Esther did when she moved from being pampered in preparation and chose to risk her own life for the benefit of others.

The time is fast approaching when we will need to draw on all of our past experiences, both the highs and the lows. The lows develop our faith and character; the highs refresh our souls and inspire us to greater things. When we experience a foretaste of what is yet to come, such as the outpouring of the Holy Spirit in renewing anointing, healing and celebration, it creates faith for our future. If what we experience here and now is marvellous we are filled with greater joy knowing that the best is yet to come. For we know that our current life is nothing in comparison to that which will be revealed in eternity.

It was at a Catch The Fire meeting in Toronto that I felt the most intense sense of the presence of God. I was standing at the front in the midst of the crowd surrounded by singing, dancing and exuberant praise. An elderly gentleman with many years of ministry and experience held me, looked straight into my eyes and said that he had never felt so close to glory in all of his life. He wondered aloud how it could possibly get any better and was ecstatic to realise that heaven would be far, far greater than anything that he was experiencing at that moment. What a foretaste of glory divine. What an encouragement. What a blessing.

✳ ✳ ✳

These glimpses of divine inspiration, moments of true encounter with the Holy Spirit, should not to be trivialised or dismissed out of hand. Such experiences will give us strength to press on in to take hold of that for which God has taken hold of us and serve as a precious foretaste of what is yet to come. My prayer is, "More Lord; more of your presence, more of your love, more of your grace." As Psalm 85:6-7 says:

"Will You not revive us again, that Your people may rejoice in You? Show us Your mercy, Lord, and grant us Your salvation."

Even Jesus needed to keep His focus on the future in order to endure the suffering of His day. Hebrews 12:2 instructs us:

"Let us fix our eyes on Jesus, the author and perfecter of our

faith, who for the joy set before Him endured the cross, scorning its shame, and sat down at the right hand of the throne of God."

How much more do we, today, need a foretaste of the future to help us endure the increasing resistance to the gospel, persecution and evil and discipline of the Refiner's fire. I think it's quite wonderful that the Holy Spirit would be willing to bring such a party to the Church. It's a little like Psalm 23 where David says:

"He prepares a table before me in the presence of my enemies."

If we are right in the midst of battle, facing our enemies, God prepares a banquet for us as a prophetic foretaste of what is yet to come. It will be the ultimate insult to the devil, an offence to the religious and an act of incredible faith when we can relax in the presence of the Father, trusting Him to be in control of His universe whilst we soak in His love and grace. When we begin to rest in and enjoy the Father, the restoration and renewal process of our lives becomes more effective. It enables us, through the Holy Spirit, to go back out into battle with our focus on the hope of the future because we have had a prophetic glimpse of that which is still to come. It is so true what the Apostle Paul said to the church at Corinth:

"What no eye has seen, what no ear has heard, and what no human mind has conceived ... the things God has prepared for those who love him..." (1 Cor 2:9)

* * *

Over the years Karen and I have learnt to try to listen to

the Holy Spirit for what is appropriate in any given situation. Seeking to hear God 'in the now' helps us not to default to doing what we have always done and assume this to be God's strategy. This is not to discredit what has worked in the past, but rather to recognise that God has a variety of ways of doing things and obeying Him in the immediate gives us a greater chance of fruitfulness and success. By way of illustration I will share one such event with you.

While pioneering a church in Lancaster, a city in the north west of England, we faced many spiritual challenges, most notably a poverty spirit that gripped the region. In part this manifested itself among the people through a fear of loss or not having enough. Resultantly, a general retentiveness was evident and small-minded thinking often controlled peoples' decision making. There were, of course, a number of faith-filled believers who had great vision and courage, but generally speaking it was an uphill struggle to inspire enthusiastic responses for faith ventures, encourage emotive worship or gain active participation in prayer. During our time there we were challenged financially and all too frequently we hit a wall of financial deficit that frustrated the realisation of the dream that God had put in our hearts. Often we would engage in seasons of prayer and fasting as part of our spiritual warfare, pressing into God when we were faced with seemingly insurmountable obstacles. Importantly, as best we could, we also tried to develop a culture of celebration. On one such difficult occasion I felt God remind me of Psalm 23:

"The Lord is my shepherd, I lack nothing. He makes me lie down in green pastures, He leads me beside quiet waters, He refreshes my soul. He guides me along the right paths for his name's sake. Even though I walk through the darkest valley, I will fear no evil, for You are with me; Your rod and Your staff, they comfort me. You prepare a table before me in the presence of my enemies. You anoint my head with oil; my cup overflows. Surely Your goodness and love will follow me all the days of my life, and I will dwell in the house of the Lord

forever."

This whole psalm is a celebration of Father's absolute commitment to His children. No matter what our circumstances it reminds us of God's amazing provision, blessing, abundance, rest and favour, even to the point of providing a banquet for us in the face of the enemy!

So it was that we decided not to go into deep agony of prayer and fasting but to declare the goodness of God and hold a party! Believing that Father was fully aware of all things, we proclaimed the truth of scripture above the reality of our circumstances and celebrated victory even before we had realised it in the natural.

Now, we need to put the resultant miracle into context! At that time the location of our church building was in the top 10% of deprived areas in our nation. Around us we witnessed generational unemployment, low ambition, a lack of care for the community and an entitlement mentality. We wanted to purchase an old Methodist church whose congregation had reduced such that they were no longer able to maintain the upkeep of their building. We had been saving for a church facility but to date had not been able to accumulate very much, nonetheless we visited the site and drove a stake into the ground, claiming it in Jesus' name. At this point two of our intercessors, who by nature were respectable, sophisticated women, both fell to the floor and started roaring with laughter, rolling around as if they were drunk! Onlookers in cars waiting at the adjacent traffic lights watched in bewilderment as this went on and eventually we managed to gather up the ladies to join the rest of us as we prayed. However others then began to be touched too, making bowing motions as they called out "Ho"! It was as if Father had released something special to us which birthed fresh faith and confidence to proceed. The story continues with the receipt of a financial miracle following a gift day, - the culmination of a series of fun faith ventures. In a single meeting we managed to raise all of the money required to purchase the building. Our cup was overflowing!

In times of battle, think about responding in the opposite spirit. Where there is retention, be generous. Where there is hate, demonstrate love. Where there is overwhelming oppression, throw a party! He prepares a table for us in the presence of our enemies! Theres nothing like a party to thwart the enemies plans and to release heaven's reality into earth's circumstances.

Obedience is key. Esther chose to obey and this led to blessing. Vashti chose to disobey and was rejected. When we hear the command of God we are faced with a choice and we set our destiny accordingly.

THE PREPARED BRIDE

Back in chapter two we started by looking at how Holy Spirit is preparing the Bride for the return of the Bridegroom. Now we will look at the finished article; the prepared Bride as revealed in Revelation 21.

Often, when we are in our planning meetings and considering a course of action, we will ask the simple question" to what end?" This is a powerful question that helps us to narrow our focus and eliminate peripheral irrelevances that might otherwise lead us off track or take up too much time and energy, distracting us from our original goals. "To what end?" is an enquiry into where a given course of action will take us? What will the end result be? How does this help or hinder us in realising our objectives?

If we want to successfully complete any project, whether we're building the Church, doing some DIY, decorating a room or cooking a meal, it is important to understand the end result before we even commence work. When we know where we are going and what we are aiming at it is far easier to plan, navigate, make adjustments, and generally direct our time, energy and resources in a fruitful manner. I believe that Revelation 21 helps us to identify the end game, the target, the ultimate purpose and vision of God for His Church. All that we do, our time, our energy, and our effort can be channelled towards realising His dream and our purpose - *The Prepared Bride*. This is the ultimate vision of God for His people and His eternal purposes.

Revelation 21 is the continuation of an unfolding revelation. John, as best as he knew how, tried to find language to describe what he saw and what he heard. He obediently wrote down the sights, sounds and experiences as he encountered them. All of them were from another world, way beyond anything he had experienced before. Whilst his account may seem alien or confusing to us today, I am sure that it felt incredibly relevant and that its meaning was clear to him and to his immediate readers, especially when taking into account the context that they were living in. I feel, however, that much of the original meaning of the imagery is lost on us today, though it is undoubtedly as important as it was two millennia past.

What John saw.

The first two verses record that John saw a new heaven and a new earth. He noticed that the old heaven and earth had passed away and that there was no longer any sea.

Traditionally the sea is symbolic of a realm of evil, full of chaos, turbulence, where man cannot survive and where monsters live. Hence, God promised land to His people. Accordingly, scripture often employs phrases and evokes images of "taking the land" or moving into" a land flowing with milk and honey". Typically such instances are synonymous with the notion of reclaiming what the enemy has stolen and restoring to us that which we have lost. In biblical imagery the idea of receiving land is a good thing because it usually encapsulates some redemptive qualities. Even when the land we receive might appear to be a wilderness we are assured that it will ultimately turn into a place of fruitfulness. For example:

"The desert and the parched land will be glad; the wilderness will rejoice and blossom...." (Isaiah 35:1)

God is intent on redeeming, restoring and healing the

land.

John sees that the sea and all that it represents is no more. As you may recall back in Revelation 20, all evil, the devil, Antichrist, Death and Hades along with all those whose names are not written in the Lambs book of life, have been thrown into the lake of fire. The sea has gone, and the old order of things has passed away.

* * *

In Revelation 21:9-11 an angel invites John to come with him so that he can show him the Bride, the wife of the Lamb. He is carried away in the Spirit to a mountain great and high. Here John is shown the Holy City, Jerusalem, coming down out of heaven from God. It shone with the glory of God, prepared like a bride for her husband.

What God is showing John is of such great importance that He reveals it to him twice. Once from where he was at the time, on earth, and then from a different vantage point, from a great and high mountain. Both viewings reveal exactly the same event but they serve multiple purposes. Firstly and simply the repetition emphasises the significance of what he was seeing. Secondly, it demonstrates that what is happening is both a heavenly and an earthly event. Perhaps this is where God's Kingdom evidently reigns - when the perspectives of heaven and earth align and are manifest as one singular reality. That is, after all, what we pray and ask for when we pray the Lord's prayer.

In Revelation 3:12 John refers to this city as the City of God. He calls it the New Jerusalem and sees it coming out of heaven from God. In Revelation 21:1-2 the Holy City, the New Jerusalem, is in fact the Church, the Bride of Christ. They are one and the same thing. The New Jerusalem is described as the wife of the Lamb, His bride, beautifully dressed for her husband.

Remember in Hebrews 11:10-16 how Abraham was confidently looking forward to the city with eternal foundations, whose architect and builder was God? He was a man of great faith. He, along with subsequent generations, looked forward to the full realisation of the revelation that they held dear in their hearts. They hadn't yet received the fulfilment of the promise in their lifetime, yet they welcomed it from a distance. They lived as strangers and aliens here in this corrupted world whilst longing for a better land – a heavenly one. Even though they wander God is not ashamed to be called their God, for He has prepared a city for them.

Today, the hope and expectation of God's people is still to enter into that land, that city, that eternal dwelling place with Jesus. The writer to the Hebrews explains that even now, in our time, we can approach that eternal dwelling for it exists in heaven and is accessible through Christ:

"But you have come to Mount Zion, to the city of the living God, the heavenly Jerusalem. You have come to thousands upon thousands of angels in joyful assembly, to the church of the firstborn, whose names are written in heaven. You have come to God, the Judge of all, to the spirits of the righteous made perfect, to Jesus the mediator of a new covenant, and to the sprinkled blood that speaks a better word than the blood of Abel." (Heb 12:22-24)

Here the City of God is called Mount Zion, the heavenly Jerusalem. It is the community of God's family. Included within this community are God, Jesus, thousands of angels, and the spirits of the righteous made perfect through our Saviour's blood, sealed into a new covenant and brought into an eternal heavenly family.

Heaven is a literal place where The Divine, the angels and the spirits of saved people dwell in a spiritual dimension. We know it is there. We know it is close. The writer of Hebrews reveals that heaven is also all around us:

"Therefore, since we are surrounded by such a great cloud of witnesses, let us throw off..." (Heb 11:1)

Through the Holy Spirit we have access to this realm right now, right here. In this sense we are already connected as one heavenly family, united in Christ and through the indwelling of His Spirit. Whilst we bodily reside and live here on earth, we know that we are simultaneously dwelling spiritually in that City with Christ (Eph 2:6). We also have faith that we will fully experience heaven and enter completely into this spiritual realm and community when we die. Yet there is a further hope still; that foreseen by John of a realm coming out of heaven to earth and replacing the old order. Currently we have but a foretaste of the heavenly reality which is yet to come. In the future we will experience the full realisation of this heavenly reality when it will be fully manifest in the natural realm.

The apostle Paul describes how he understood the future coming of heaven to earth in a real and tangible sense.

"Brothers and sisters, we do not want you to be uninformed about those who sleep in death, so that you do not grieve like the rest of mankind, who have no hope. For we believe that Jesus died and rose again, and so we believe that God will bring with Jesus those who have fallen asleep in him. According to the Lord's word, we tell you that we who are still alive, who are left until the coming of the Lord, will certainly not precede those who have fallen asleep. For the Lord himself will come down from heaven, with a loud command, with the voice of the archangel and with the trumpet call of God, and the dead in Christ will rise first. After that, we who are still alive and are left will be caught up together with them in the clouds to meet the Lord in the air. And so we will be with the Lord forever. Therefore encourage one another with these words" (1 Thess 4:13-18)

We see here the Lord Himself, along with angels, coming out of heaven to earth. At His command the dead in Christ will be raised and those who are alive at that time will, along with them, be caught up to be with the Lord to meet Him at His coming. This gathering of the family of faith includes the resurrection of the dead. Paul describes this event further:

"Listen, I tell you a mystery: We will not all sleep, but we will all be changed—in a flash, in the twinkling of an eye, at the last trumpet. For the trumpet will sound, the dead will be raised imperishable, and we will be changed. For the perishable must clothe itself with the imperishable, and the mortal with immortality." (1 Cor 15:51-53)

Christ's return will be such an amazing and wonderful event. It will include the supernatural, instant fulfilment of many promises. Christ will come from heaven to earth, there will be a heavenly trumpet blast, the voice of the archangel and the command of Christ will resound for all to hear. Those whose spirits have been dwelling with Christ in heaven will enter their newly resurrected bodies and those alive at this time will, along with them, be given immortal bodies. An utter transformation. A complete realisation of all we have hoped and believed for. All mortality, pain, suffering, corruption and death will fall away in an instant. We will be clothed in our new resurrected bodies, free, whole, holy, healthy, and at one with our precious Saviour and Lord Jesus Christ.

Was John seeing this cataclysmic event from a fresh and alternate perspective? Did he receive insights and details different to that which Paul had received? I believe they saw the same thing from two different perspectives, each bringing to the table a piece of the jigsaw of revelation so that we might see the whole picture in far greater clarity. I am confident that Abraham, too, saw in his spirit the same culmination of the dream of God for the fulfilment of His promises. As detailed in Hebrews 11, and along with the other hero's of faith, Abraham longed for this day - the realisation of a city designed and prepared by God.

John saw the apotheosis of the ages, the fulfilment of all prophecy, the actual realisation of our Father's dream made manifest. The Church, the Bride made ready and coming to earth, beautifully dressed for her husband the Lord Jesus Christ.

What did John hear?

From Revelation 21:3 we read that John heard a loud voice emanating from the throne. The throne is the ultimate seat of authority. It symbolises kingly power, dominance and dignity. It is the position from which a realm is ruled. It is certainly an exalted position for the one who sits on the throne. When Isaiah...

"... saw the Lord seated on a throne, high and exalted, and the train of His robe filled the temple..." (Isa 6:1)

... he caught a glimpse from earth into the heavenly realm and encountered the Exalted One. All of heaven worshipped Him. Angels covered their faces, so glorious is the presence of the One on the throne. They cried to one another," holy, holy, holy, is the LORD Almighty." The whole temple shook at the sound of their voices. Now that is loud! That is powerful! Smoke filled the temple. This has to illustrate His presence and His glory. Isaiah, totally overwhelmed, declared that he was falling apart at such a revelation! He became utterly convicted of his own unworthiness to be in the presence of such holiness and magnificence.

The prophet Zachariah (Zach 6:13) speaks of the LORD who will sit and rule on His throne. We understand that the throne of King David represented the throne of God. This is made clear when Solomon, David's son, sat on his father's throne.

"So Solomon sat on the throne of the LORD as king in place of his father David." (1 Chron 29:23)

Whoever sat on the throne ruled on behalf of God.

Amazingly, Isaiah saw clearly the connection between David's throne and the coming Messiah. David sat upon a throne and ruled on behalf of God for but a moment, but Christ comes, sat upon a high and exalted throne, and rules on behalf of God for all of eternity.

*"For to us a child is born, to us a son is given, and the government will be on his shoulders. And he will be called Wonderful Counsellor, Mighty God, Everlasting Father, Prince of Peace. Of the greatness of his government and peace there will be no end. **He will reign on David's throne and over his kingdom** establishing and upholding it with justice and righteousness from that time on and forever....."* (Isaiah 9:6-7)

The New Testament refers to Jesus as the Son of the Most High who sits on the throne of David.

"He will be great and will be called the Son of the Most High. The Lord God will give Him the throne of his father David, and He will reign over the house of Jacob forever; His kingdom will never end." (Luke 1:32-33)

This concept of thrones continues throughout the New Testament. Paul writes to the Ephesian church about Christ:

*"... his incomparably great power for us who believe. That power is the same as the mighty strength he exerted when he raised Christ from the dead and **seated him at his right hand in the heavenly realms**, far above all rule and authority, power and dominion, and every name that is invoked, not only in the present age but also in the one to come."* (Rev 1:19-21)

Christ is seated at the right hand of Almighty God in the heavenly realms. In this exalted position, upon a throne, Christ is far above and superior to all rule, authority, power and dominion. Everything is subject to Him.

Moreover, having been saved by Christ from sin and its consequences, Paul also notes that we are now seated with Him in the heavenly realms (Ephesians 2:6). So not only has Christ risen, ascended and been seated upon His throne, He's also provided a way for us to sit alongside and rule with Him.

This imagery continues in Revelation chapter 4. John, having received revelation for the churches, proceeds to tell us that he saw a door open before him. In response to a voice inviting him "up here" he was at once in the spirit. John tries his utmost to describe what he saw. Before him was a throne in heaven, encircled by the glow of an emerald. Someone who shone with brilliance was sitting upon it. Around this throne were twenty-four other thrones where elders were seated. From the central throne came flashes of lightening and rumblings of thunder. Seven torches with burning flames were before the throne, in addition to what looked like a sea of glass which sparkled like a crystal. Four living beings were around the centre throne, crying day and night:

"Holy, holy, holy is the Lord God Almighty, who was, who is and who is yet to come." (Rev 4:8)

Whenever these creatures gave thanks and praise the twenty-four elders fell down in worship. They laid their own crowns before the throne and said:

"You are worthy, our Lord and God, to receive honour and power, for you created all things, and by your will they were created and have their being." (Rev 4:11)

Wow! What a sight. what a revelation of the heavenly

realm! John saw so much of what is going on around the throne of heaven. Take time to re-read Revelation chapters 4 and 5 for yourself and marvel at what John saw. All of this speaks of the magnificence of the throne and its pre-eminence in heaven over everything that surrounds it. Everything praises and worships the One who sits upon the throne with total adoration, gratitude, submission and awe.

* * *

Whilst this picture was certainly an accurate representation of what was going on in heaven at the time John saw it, it would be my belief that this is still what is taking place in heaven right now, in this moment, even though we are unaware of it here on earth.

In Revelation 21:3 John hears a loud voice coming from the throne. Presumably the one seated on the throne is the one communicating. You may notice that 'loud' does seem to be a recurring mode of communication in heaven. According to the book of Revelation we read about loud voices, shouts, loud trumpets and cries! There are in fact 258 accounts of God's people using a loud voice in the bible. I think the idea here is obvious - the voice is lifted to garner attention, to cut out distraction and to ensure that it is being heard above all other noises. In John's particular instance the voice is essentially saying: "Now that I've got your attention you need to hear what I am communicating because it's of vital importance. You need to listen and take heed."

This is what the voice from the throne said to John:

"Now the dwelling of God is with men, and He will live with them. They will be His people. God himself will be with them and be their

God."

These three statements affirm God's abiding presence with a people that He calls His own.

Note that there are past, present and future components to the revelation that John is experiencing. In Revelation John often refers to the past ("I know your deeds…"), to the present ("Repent, do not be afraid, wake up!") and to the future ("I will give right to eat from the tree of life, I will give manna, I will give a white stone" etc.)

It is interesting to note that the voice in Revelation 21:3 begins with "Now!", or in other translations "Look!" The voice is focusing on what is taking place in the present moment.

At the beginning of the book of Revelation Jesus tells John:

"Write therefore what you have seen, <u>what is now</u> and what will take place later." (Rev 1:19)

When Holy Spirit speaks of "now" there is of course a "now" in the very present sense, the immediate, this moment in time. There are also statements of "now" that have future connotations. The writer is seeing an event which has yet to come to fruition. He is foreseeing what it yet to transpire.

By way of example, in Revelation 4 John describes how he saw an open door in heaven and a voice speaking like a trumpet saying *"Come up here, and I will show you what must take place after."* John immediately sees into heaven and views what is probably beyond earthly time constraints. He is shown images beyond his imagination, revealing Christ, heavenly creatures, worshipping saints, angels and things that are yet to take place.

I am confident that each revelation had an immediate relevancy to the first hearers of John's vision. John's revelation was depicted in vivid imagery that expresses the reality of both spiritual and natural warfare. It would have inspired and encouraged his listeners because they faced gross persecution from many sides and were enduring the oppression of the Roman empire. Yet his vision also highlights what is yet to be fulfilled and realised. Hence the book of Revelation didn't just resonate with the early church, it is incredibly relevant for us today and for the church of the future.

Having heard the loud voice from the throne speaking to him, John records for us the words he heard:

"Now the dwelling of God is with men, and He will live with them."
"They will be His people."
"God himself will be with them and be their God."

We understand and believe God dwells with us "now" by His Holy Spirit. We are known as God's people and He is willing for us to represent Him. He is our God who is with us in a very literal sense. However, this voice is also speaking of what is yet to come, yet to be fully realised when Jesus Himself returns to planet earth again in physical form along with the host of heaven. The "now" in the immediate moment of time is a fore-taste of what is yet to be completed when the "now" of the future becomes our present reality.

The presence of the divine abiding with us brings about amazing benefits. The voice from the throne declares that:

"He will wipe away every tear from their eyes."
"There will be no more death or mourning or crying or pain."

This is more than merely a future hope. This promised comfort is also part of our a present reality. We constantly experience the amazing work of the Holy Spirit bringing healing to our spirit, soul and body through the ministry of the church. In the future, when heaven is fully realised here on earth, there will be no more suffering, death, mourning, crying or pain. Jesus will have wiped away the tears of every memory of trauma, cruelty, injustice, misunderstanding, brokenness, humiliation and shame. Until then we minister healing and deliverance as best as we are able, under the anointing of the Holy Spirit, in Jesus' name. In the kingdom to come there will be no more suffering, sickness, disease or damage in the human experience. Until then we heal, comfort, encourage and give hope. In the kingdom to come there will be no more sin, no more demonic activity and no more Satan. Until then we cast out demons in Jesus' name and share the gospel of Christ to bring salvation from Satan, sin and its damaging consequences.

The voice of the one who sat on the throne continues:

"The old order of things has passed away."
"I am making everything new!"

Again, this has present and future ramifications.

Paul said the to the Corinthian church,

"Therefore, if anyone is in Christ, the new creation has come: The old has gone, the new is here!" (2 Cor 5:17)

This is our present reality. Those of us who are in Christ have become a new creation. Our sin has been washed away by the blood of Jesus, the Holy Spirit now lives in us and we are eternally saved by faith in Christ. We have been born again; we have started a new life. We have left behind all the shame, guilt and pain of the past to begin a new life empowered by the abiding presence of Christ in us. We still battle with our old nature but with the help of the Holy Spirit we overcome temptation and embrace the process of being transformed and conformed into the image of Christ. The old has gone, the new creation has begun in our lives.

This all culminates and is perfected when Jesus returns and makes everything new. The old order of things is done away with along with Satan, Jezebel, death and Hades and all works of darkness that work against the throne of God and seek to destroy all that is love, holy, righteous and just. Judgement falls

145

on all forms of rebellion, wickedness and evil. Christ ushers in a new world order.

I believe this new world order is depicted in the image of the Holy City, the New Jerusalem, coming out of heaven prepared as a bride beautifully dressed for her husband. In once sense the Bride has come already because the Church exist here now, expressing and manifesting the kingdom of God, declaring good news and bringing light into darkness. However this is merely a foretaste of what is to be fully realised when Christ returns. The season that we are in at this present moment is for the preparation of the Bride, the Church, in anticipation of the Bridegroom and the Bride become one in a very literal and tangible reality.

What did John have to do?

John was instructed to write down what he saw and heard. Indeed the message is so important that the voice of the one seated upon the throne wants him to record all that he sees and hears, for what he is about to hear is:

"Trustworthy and true." (Rev 21:5)

By doing so each subsequent generation of God's people would be able to read about and hear God's voice for themselves, inspiring hope, life and faith.

This is what John had wrote down:

"It is done. I am the Alpha and the Omega, the beginning and the end. To him who is thirsty I will give him to drink without cost from the spring of life. To him who overcomes will inherit all this. I will be his God and he will be my son."

This declaration identifies the one who sits on the throne as the Alpha and Omega, the beginning and the end. This is the

Christ who was from the beginning of time and is unto eternity united as one with the Father.

"In the beginning was the Word and the Word was with God and the Word was God. He was with God in the beginning. Through [Christ] all things were made..." (John 1:1-3)

John is affirming the eternal existence of Christ, His equality and union with the Father, and His active role in the creation of all things. This confirms the identity of voice from the throne: Jesus the Christ speaking. He is establishing who He is and revealing the authority that He has.

He announces that His work has been fully and eternally accomplished. *"It is done!"* The ultimate dream in the heart of the Divine has been fully realised. The whole of history, as we understand it, is satisfied and bursts into a new age. We see this proclamation paralleled on the cross when Jesus cried out *"It is finished"* (John 19:30) to signify the completion of His earthly ministry and to provide atonement for sinful humankind. He has worked redemption, reconciliation and propitiation through His death on the cross.

Finally, Christ tells John to write down that those who overcome will inherit all of this, and I will be their God and they will be my children. Again, this is both a promise and a current reality. Paul teaches us through his letter to the Romans that:

"Those who are led by the Spirit of God are the sons of God."

And again he says that:

"The Holy Spirit testifies with our human spirit that we are sons of God. If we are sons then we are also heirs of the father and co-heirs with Jesus himself." (Rom 8:14-17)

Because Christ's work is finished we can receive salvation immediately. We are now sons of the Father, able to live in the reality of being an heir. We can be filled with His Holy Spirit if we are thirsty and this Spirit gives us the power and authority to overcome, conquer, subdue and be victorious over sin and the works of darkness. It also says that we can, by His grace, represent, reflect and operate on His behalf as true sons of the Father, right now. All of this is a foretaste of what is yet to be fully realised when Jesus comes and establishes His Kingdom in full reality on earth. Until then we can live on the earth drawing upon the heavenly resources secured for us in Christ Jesus. In fact Paul tells us that the whole of creation is eagerly waiting for the sons of God to be revealed (Romans 8:19) and that when they do:

"Creation itself will be liberated from its bondage to decay and brought into the glorious freedom of the sons of God" (Rom 8:21)

Romans 8:22 informs us that at this present moment the whole of creation is groaning, as if it were in labour awaiting childbirth. To think that creation is tired of its suffering, decay and its corrupt nature due to the consequences of sin, and it is longing for, in fact crying out for, the true sons of God to rise up and be made manifest so that it too may enter into the benefits of true freedom found in Christ Jesus. This is an ongoing process and will become more apparent as we near the time of Christ's return.

However...

Revelation 21:8 clearly states that whilst some people are being prepared as the Bride of Christ, others will not enter into union with the Bridegroom when He returns. The voice from the throne lists those who are not included:

"The cowardly, the unbelieving, the murderers, the sexually immoral, those who practice magic arts, the idolaters, and all liars -

their fate is the fiery lake of burning sulphur." (Rev 21:8)

Tragic. Terrifying. Yet a reality. Those who reject Christ, His salvation and offer of acceptance and continue to live a life that rebels against all that is holy and right, not according to mankind's standards but by God's standards, will be rejected and suffer the consequences of their unforgiven sin. Time will have run out and only those who are found in Christ, those who form part of the Bride, will be saved.

This is confirmed in Revelation 22:14-15 when Christ contrasts those who are in and those who are outside of His kingdom. Here Jesus tells us that it is those who have washed their robes, another way of saying those who have been cleansed from sin and now wear robes of Christ righteousness, these people are able to enter this glorious city and have the right to the tree of life. Conversely, those who are outside of the city and cannot enter are those who are unregenerate, lost souls. The list is similar to what Jesus has already illustrated. The Murderers, idolaters, those who practice magic arts, the sexually immoral and those who practice falsehood.

This is another example of a present reality that will be fully realised in eternity. Those who are in Christ can enter the city of God, also known as the house of the Lord, the Body of Christ, the New Jerusalem, Zion, the true Church. Those who are not in Christ are not in the Church; not in the city, nor can they enter it. I am confident that there will be a clearer distinction between these two groups as we see the final days of the old order of things approaching.

The environment of the city.

This New Jerusalem is built according to very exact measurements. In Revelation 21 we see that it has twelve gates, three on each of its four sides. Each gate is made from a single pearl. The walls were made from various precious gems and gold. The great street within the city is made from pure gold and is transparent like glass.

Verse 22 tells us that there is no temple in the city because the Lord God almighty and the lamb are its temple. No temple. No building serving as the focal point of corporate worship. No place for sacrifice. The need of the temple has been done away with, for Christ has fulfilled the Levitical laws associated with the priesthood. Christ is now the object of worship and the focal point of devotion. He is living in the midst of His people, the Church, the Bride, the New Jerusalem, the Holy City. His presence and His glory is the light in the City. The Lamb is the lamp. This is why we read in verse 23:

"The city does not need the sun or the moon to shine on it, for the glory of God gives it light, and the Lamb is its lamp." (Rev 21:23)

This abiding presence of the Divine in the midst of His people gives light to all who are in Christ Jesus. It exudes out of the Body of Christ into the world.

"Again Jesus spoke to them, saying, "I am the light of the world. Whoever follows me will not walk in darkness, but will have the light of life." (John 8:12)

Revelation 21:24 tells us that:

"The nations will walk by its light and the Kings of the earth will bring their splendour to it."

The nations of the world have undoubtedly benefitted immensely from the light of the Kingdom of Heaven being made manifest through civilisation, law, education, medicine, science, welfare, moral law, human rights etc. The Church has preserved and proclaimed the gospel of Christ and sought to present and reveal Jesus as the true light of the world.

All of this speaks of the immediate reality of this vision.

It reveals the role and influence of the church throughout history until the present day. This truth and function is confirmed in so many other places in scriptures, not just here in Revelation. Yet, once again, we will step into a more complete realisation of all of this when Christ returns to receive His Bride unto Himself.

We notice from verse 25 on that the gates into the city will never be shut. Only those whose names are in the lambs book of life will be able to enter into the city. Nothing impure will ever enter it nor will anyone who does what is shameful or deceitful. This reaffirms what John saw earlier in verse 8, that those outside of Christ have no place nor way of entering into the Holy City, now or in the future.

What's in the city? (Revelation 22)

John is led by an angel and shown inside the city. He sees the river of life flowing from the throne of God down the middle of the great street in the city. On either side of the river stood the tree of life. He observes that the tree of life bears twelve crops of fruit which it yields every month, and that its leaves are for the healing of the nations.

Once again this is an illustration of the life of God in the midst of the Bride, His Church. The Holy Spirit flows from the throne of Christ into the heart of the Church and through His people. The fruit of the Holy Spirit is manifest and its influence brings healing to individuals and to nations.

John perceived that there was no longer any curse in this city, for all curse has been dealt with by Christ upon the cross. Instead, we have become the object of Divine blessing. This blessing is accessible right now by faith, yet the time will come when we will enter into the full manifestation of complete and total blessing.

Here in the city sits the throne of God and the Lamb. The servants of the Lamb serve He who sits on the throne and they will see His face! And His name will be on their foreheads. Oh my, to see His face as we see one another is going to be a joy unspeakable, an experience beyond anything we have hitherto encountered! To look into the eyes of the One who created us, gave us life, redeemed us, purposed us and lives to constantly bless us with His love and acceptance. To see Him in all reality and to know Him even as we are known. I am sure we will be caught up and lost in awe and wonder as we gaze upon Him. We will also have His seal of ownership upon our lives. He will mark our foreheads with His own name to indicate to whom we belong. With this direct access to the Father and His seal upon us we will be able to rule and reign with Christ forever.

John describes how all forms of darkness have now gone and that the divine light of Christ fills the whole city. There's no need for lamps or lights, sun or moon because His presence and glory radiates from the throne and gives light to all within the city.

Finally, we have the very words of Jesus from verse 12 declaring that He is coming soon and with Him is His reward that will be given to each one for that which they have done. His people will have open access to enter the city and have the right to partake in the tree of life.

As I keep reiterating, all of this vision has two components - a present reality and a future fulfilment. Paul speaks eloquently in Ephesians chapter 2 about Christ being seated on the throne in the heavenly realms above all rule and authority and that we too, having been saved through grace, are also seated with Him in the heavenly realms. We are with Him now, in the spirit, seated with Him in heaven. Paul expresses forcefully that we are blessed already, with every spiritual blessing in Christ (Ephesians 1:3). This is all a reality now. We need to grasp this truth if we are going to rise up as true sons of God. We must seek wisdom to know how to access and enter into the reality of this in the here and now. This is a foretaste of what is yet to be fully manifest in eternity.

This is, I believe, what John saw. The reality of who Christ is and who we are in Christ. He saw the Bride coming out of heaven down to earth. He saw the immediate reality of the true Church becoming all that he was seeing and hearing. He was shown the complete fulfilment, the magnificent realisation and culmination of the ages. The darkness and all it represents is gone: Death; evil; sorrow; suffering; decay etc. He saw the new age dawning. Christ's return ushering in heaven on earth with all its benefits and blessings. He saw the glory of Christ and the whole of creation bowing and worshipping Him on the throne, rightly sovereign and exercising rule with absolute love, grace and true justice. Jesus the Christ dwelling with His Bride, prepared for rulership alongside the Bridegroom, reflecting, representing and extending His kingdom. Together one for eternity in everlasting peace, displaying the unimaginable magnificence of the Divine.

CONCLUSION

Jesus is coming again and the Father has released the Holy Spirit to prepare the Bride, - us, for the return of His Son, Jesus. There are four key areas which I understand the Holy Spirit to be emphasising as He lines us up with His agenda for His Church. These are; intimacy, holiness, healing and equipping. The shape of Church is changing to embrace, develop and express these priorities which lie on the heart of God for the preparation of the Bride.

Holy Spirit is winning our hearts and ruining us for anything other than Him, by His love and grace he is drawing us closer, revealing more of who He is and impressing us with His presence. He desires to soak us in the Father's love and anointing. Instead of trying to gain His approval and acceptance, we can now serve Him from a position of security and assurance, fulfilling His plans and purposes. Intimacy is high on God's agenda. He is calling us back to a first love just as He did to the church in Ephesus (Revelation 2).

Our quest for endless programmes, overactivity, structures and strategies, whilst these are important to function well, may become idols when they replace the person Jesus and the relationship we are designed to have with Him. Jesus is no longer the means to an end, - the blesser, provider, power supplier. He is the end in Himself. He becomes the object of our love and devotion; not a means to realise a vision or accomplish an objective, no matter how honourable. He is causing us to fall in love with Him all over again and re-lay foundations on which He can build our lives. This is essential because the whole of creation is longing for the revelation of the Sons of God so that it too may enter into the glorious freedom (Romans 8:19, 21). It is time for the true Sons of the Father, the Bride of Christ, to realise who we are in Christ, to know and enter into the experience of divine love, overwhelmed by grace and motivated by divine vision. These true Sons are atmosphere changers, influencers, releasers of life, but this can only become a reality if we have been radically transformed by the Father's love. In turn this will motivate and cause us to love others even as the Father loves us.

* * *

God is a Holy God and He is preparing His Church to be holy for the return of the Lord Jesus. This is a prophetic foretaste of the holiness we will know when we are one with Him. The apostle Paul reveals this glorious hope of the church:

"Listen, I tell you a mystery: We will not all sleep, but we will all be changed in a flash, in the twinkling of an eye, at the last trumpet. For the trumpet will sound, the dead will be raised imperishable, and we will be changed. For the perishable must clothe itself with the imperishable, and the mortal with immortality." (1 Cor 15:51-53).

Until this happens we are on a journey of transformation whereby Holy Spirit is committed to purging, cleansing and calling us to holiness:

"Blessed are the pure in heart for they will see God." (Matt 5:6)

Holiness is the nature of God and we will become more

like Him as we draw closer to Him. He impresses the weight of His glory upon us and leaves the hallmark of His presence on our lives.

When we are refined, it is not a punishment but a process of conforming us into a greater image and likeness of Jesus Christ. Bearing His nature, His character, His presence lifts us to a place where we carry a true authority and move under a powerful anointing because we reflect a Christlikeness in holiness, purity and glory. It was this light that the demons saw and screamed in terror when confronted by Christ. It was this abiding presence of holiness that convicts of sin and brings about repentance. We are called to true holiness so that our lives reflect and represent Christ well.

❋ ❋ ❋

Healing and wholeness are part of our ministry here on earth; an expression of Father's deep love, power and grace, prophetically pointing towards complete wholeness in Christ. The Bible tells us that when He returns we will have incorruptible bodies, just like His, and we will be perfect, just as He is perfect. Until then we heal the sick, cast out demons and preach the gospel, bringing about a transformation as truth enters hearts and minds and revealing a foretaste of what is yet to come.

Father is committed to healing us on the inside and in our physical bodies because it demonstrates who He is and establishes His power and authority. It demonstrates His reality and divinity and through healing our lives reveal the glory of God. Healing, in all its fulness, including deliverance, fulfils the biblical revelation that:

"Jesus came to destroy the works of the devil." (1 John 3:8)

We are called to share in His victory and actively destroy the works of darkness, including sickness and disease, wherever and whenever we encounter them. The very heart of God is to bring restoration to broken, damaged lives. Psalm 23 says:

"He restores our soul."

He loves to rebuild lives, freeing us, body, soul and spirit, from the adverse effects of life.

Ultimately, Father is full of compassion. This is expressed in Christ when He was asked if He was willing to heal a man who had leprosy. "I am willing", He said, "Be clean." The Father's motive is love and He is the healer. It is in His very name, Jehovah Rapha, - the Lord who mends and repairs.

✳ ✳ ✳

Finally, I see Holy Spirit preparing the Bride in these days by raising up an equipped end time army of true sons of the Father. Not only willing to serve, but trained, equipped and tested, ready to engage in a battle for the lost. An army that has moved on from emotionally charged concepts of victory into the reality of overcoming and taking territory for the advancement of the Kingdom of God.

I see true apostles, prophets, evangelists, pastors and teachers, along with intercessors, helpers, musicians and singers, counsellors, tradesman, administrators and so many more who have given wholly of themselves for the building up of the Church and the extension of His Kingdom. It will take an army of loving, self-sacrificing, courageous men and women, young and old, a body where each of us is committed to the cause of Christ, doing what we are gifted and able to do in order to complete the work of God in our generation.

On our watch, let us rise up, take our place and allow Holy Spirit to empower us and lead us into great exploits. We must know our God and give ourselves unconditionally to the One who has saved us and chosen us to rule and reign with Him throughout eternity. It's time to embrace true holiness and hunger for intimacy with the Divine, be healed of our past wounds and submit fully to the work of the Holy Spirit, even when that means having fun in His presence! We must present ourselves ready and willing to be equipped so we that can be at our best for the glory of God and the extension of His Kingdom.

Are you willing to change, humble yourselves and become childlike in your responses to God, so that He might prepare you to meet with Him?

1 Thessalonians 4:13-18 says:

"Brothers, we do not want you to be ignorant about those who fall asleep, or to grieve like the rest of men, who have no hope. We believe that Jesus died and rose again and so we believe that God will bring with Jesus those who have fallen asleep in Him. According to the Lord's own Word, we who are still alive and are left till the coming of the Lord, will certainly not precede those who have fallen asleep. For the Lord Himself will come down from heaven with a loud command, with the voice of the archangel and with the trumpet call of God, and the dead in Christ will rise first. After that, we who are still alive and are left will be caught up together with them in the clouds to meet the Lord in the air. And so we will be with the Lord forever. Therefore encourage each other with these words."

✽ ✽ ✽

ACKNOWLEDGEMENT

There are many to whom I am grateful for their help in writing this book. Especially my wife, Karen, for her ability to juggle so many balls in the air and yet take time to turn my stammering gibberish into something reasonably coherent.

For my son, Joshua. A constant companion, source of wisdom and information on all things philosophical, religious, scientific, sporting and political, who has assisted with the editing.

My prayer shield who have covered my back and battled in the heavenly realms to enable breakthroughs time and again, and those who minister as part of the R.E.A.P. team who have tirelessly journeyed and served with me through the years, travelling the length and breadth of this country and overseas. For your faithfulness, commitment, friendship and endurance I want to say thank you and acknowledge that without you what has been accomplished would never have happened. Your obvious devotion to Jesus shines through in all that you do and in the way that you do it. You know who you are so be blessed! Together we have seen so much of God's manifest love and power but your greater reward is yet to come.

Printed in Great Britain
by Amazon

86862642R00092